AN OUTLINE OF ENGLISH EDUCATION

1760—1902

BY

JOHN WILLIAM ADAMSON

EMERITUS PROFESSOR, UNIVERSITY OF LONDON

Reprinted from THE CAMBRIDGE HISTORY OF ENGLISH LITERATURE

CAMBRIDGE
AT THE UNIVERSITY PRESS
1925

CAMBRIDGE
UNIVERSITY PRESS
LONDON : Fetter Lane

BOMBAY, CALCUTTA and
MADRAS
Macmillan and Co., Ltd.
TORONTO
The Macmillan Co. of
Canada, Ltd.
TOKYO
Maruzen-Kabushiki-Kaisha

Copyrighted in the
United States of America
by G. P. Putnam's Sons

PREFACE

THE growing interest in the nineteenth century history of English education has suggested that a separate issue of Chapter XIV of the fourteenth volume of the *Cambridge History of English Literature*, here reprinted, would be of assistance to the student. The chapter covers the period, 1760–1902; but since "the nineteenth century" in this connexion may fairly be said to begin in 1789, or even earlier, the chapter is reproduced in full. It is a continuation of that on the same subject in Volume IX of the *History*, which brought the story from the early seventeenth century to 1760; and there are incidental passages in different volumes of that work which bear upon the history of education. It has therefore been thought advisable to retain the footnote references to such passages, although a consultation of the latter is not essential to the understanding of the present chapter. The bibliography will be found helpful to those for whom an outline is insufficient.

J. W. A.

August, 1925.

EDUCATION

THE latter half of the eighteenth century was marked by an hitherto unprecedented development of science. Mathematics, physics and astronomy made notable advances, the foundations of modern chemistry were laid, the idea of biological evolution was being carefully studied a century before the appearance of Darwin's *Origin of Species* (1859); the speculations of the early French economists were focused in Adam Smith's *Wealth of Nations* (1776). But the most striking results of scientific research and experiment were to be found in the applied sciences and in mechanical inventions. From the later years of George II onwards, there was an extraordinary growth in the number of labour-saving machines, more especially of those employed in the cotton and woollen industries, inventions which multiplied almost incalculably the resources of the manufacturing districts of the north and middle of England. On the heels of these inventions came the work of great engineers, Watt, Boulton, Rennie, Stephenson. The enormous economy of labour, the much greater mechanical precision of the output and the increased facility of transport, all combined to bring about an industrial expansion, which, assisted by the commercial activity of the earlier part of the century, was deep enough and broad enough to merit the name 'revolution.' Amidst such circumstances, it was inevitable that the critics of contemporary education should condemn its almost absolute disregard of useful knowledge and of modern studies.

A new people and a new order of civilised society appeared. Population increased, great urban communities arose in the midlands and in northern England, there was a general movement away from the rural districts; a hitherto unwonted aggregation of capital altered the scale of industrial operations. While wealth increased, so, also, did poverty; it would be difficult to parallel in the previous history of England the wretched state of the labouring poor during the last years of the eighteenth and the first decades of the nineteenth century. The educational provision for the mass of English children in charity, parish and Sunday schools was very insufficient, and commonly unsuitable in character. The desperate plight of parents and the unsparing employment of children in mills and factories would, in many cases, have made the offer of a complete provision little more than a mockery. Yet, these very conditions of ignorance and of moral degradation stirred the hearts of reformers to attempt their alleviation by means of schools. The evils and their remedy are both described by Wordsworth in the last two books of *The Excursion* (1795—1814).

The activity directed to educational affairs, which has been a prominent feature of English life during recent years, dates from the time of the French revolution; but, at the moment of that outbreak, France and Germany could look back upon a whole generation engaged in revolutionising national education. By the publication of *La Nouvelle Héloïse* (1761), Rousseau had protested against the prevailing rationalism, and, in the following year, he produced *Émile*, a book whose destructive and constructive proposals combined to make it the most considerable work of the eighteenth century dealing with its subject. La Chalotais and Basedow had enunciated the administrative principles of the lay school and undenominational religious teaching, while the attacks upon the Society of Jesus and its eventual suppression by papal bull in 1773 had suspended the labours of the greatest educational corporation of the time, and had inflicted a fatal blow upon the type of instruction which, for some two and a half centuries, had been general throughout Europe. Prussia, under the guidance of K. A. von Zedlitz, Frederick the great's minister of education, had initiated reforms, which made her, in this respect, the model for the German people. So early as 1763, Frederick had decreed compulsory instruction and the provision of primary schools; ten years later, F. E. von Rochow had shown how rural schools of that order could be usefully conducted. In 1781, the modern German classical school, pursuing a course of study not confined to Latin and Greek, came into being with the curriculum which Gedike introduced in Berlin. Within the same decade, Prussian schools other than primary passed from ecclesiastical control to that of a specially constituted board of education, and, by the institution (1789) of the 'leaving examination,' the first advance was made in the evolution of the modern German university.

Austria and other regions of catholic Germany had entered upon a path of reform with purposes similar to those of Prussia; but these steps were rapidly retraced during the reaction which followed the events of 1789 in France. Outside Germany, but amidst a German-speaking population, Pestalozzi had completed the inconclusive experiment in rural education which he had been conducting upon his farm, Neuhof (1774—80).

The philosophy, psychology and, in a less degree, the educational doctrines which Europe had learned from John Locke lay behind the greater part of this strenuous activity; yet the external history of English education during the period 1760—90 exhibits a complete contrast with that of her continental neighbours. Oxford, Cambridge and the public schools, as a whole, were educating a smaller number of men and boys than had resorted to them in the days of Anne. At Oxford, in the first quarter of the eighteenth century, the number of boys admitted often exceeded 300; it never reached that number between 1726 and 1810, while it often fell below 200 in the mid-century[1]. A similar decline occurred at Cambridge, and at both universities there was a fall in the number of those who graduated, which is not fully accounted for by the diminished tale of freshmen.

An agitation for the relaxation of all formal professions of religious belief had been carried on since the middle of the century by a numerically small but active group of clergymen. At the universities, the movement led to repeated attempts between 1771 and 1787 to free bachelors of arts from subscription to the Thirty-Nine Articles or from a statement of adherence to the church of England. These attempts failed, and, as a consequence, Oxford and Cambridge degrees remained closed to the conscientious dissenter, whose membership of a college could only be maintained, if at all, by subterfuge.

The statutory exercises for degrees represented a system of education which had long been obsolete, and the toleration of a merely formal compliance with the requirements had reduced the exercises to farce[2]. The proportion of fellow-commoners and gentlemen-commoners amongst the undergraduates was large; and, as a class, these young men of birth and wealth furnished an element of idleness and dissipation which only intensified evils

---

[1] Brodrick, G. C., *Memorials of Merton College.*

[2] These are described, with some natural exaggeration of phrase, in a *locus classicus* of Knox, Vicesimus, *Essays, Moral and Literary* (1782), vol. i, pp. 331 ff., ' On some parts of the discipline in our English universities.'

already too common in both universities. Vicesimus Knox, who was at Oxford from 1771 to 1778, and fellow of St John's college from 1775, asserted, in his *Liberal Education* (1781), that to send a son to either university without the safeguard of a private tutor would probably 'make shipwreck of his learning, his morals, his health and his fortune.' Yet boys of fifteen often became undergraduates. Many of the professors never lectured, and some did not make up for the omission by advancing knowledge in other ways. Those of them who did offer this compensation might fairly urge that the business of instructing the majority of those *in statu pupillari* was efficiently performed by the college tutors. The others were not likely to feel abashed in a predominantly clerical society where the pluralist and the absentee holder of a benefice were familiar figures. But the neglect of teaching by those whom the university had especially appointed for that purpose was the consequence of a process—the supersession of the university by its colleges—which had been going on for two centuries. Concurrently, Oxford and Cambridge, for the greater number of their residents, were becoming places of education rather than seats of learning. The change is reflected in *A Letter to Lord North*, which Knox addressed to the Oxford chancellor in 1789. This pamphlet suggested the intervention of parliament, and advocated a stricter discipline, a diminution of personal expenses, the strengthening of the collegiate system, an increase in the number of college tutors, the cost to be met by doubling tuition fees and abolishing 'useless' professors, with confiscation of their endowments. College tutors were to exercise a parental control over their pupils, and professors not of the 'useless' order were to lecture thrice weekly in every term, or resign. Long after this letter was written, Cambridge undergraduates who broke rules were subject to the schoolboy punishment of 'learning lines' by heart.

But, even in this period of stagnation, reformers and some reforms were not wanting within the universities themselves. At Cambridge, the written examinations held in the Senate house reduced the ancient exercises in the schools to mere forms of no intrinsic importance; although the latter survived till 1839, the Senate house examination from 1780 onwards set the standard and determined the direction of academic study. At this time, there was but one tripos, the examination including natural religion, moral philosophy and 'Locke' as well as mathematics, the last being the dominant and characteristic part of the test; some contemporary critics believed that the effect of the tripos upon schools was to depreciate classical, in favour of mathematical learning[1]. Between 1773 and 1776, John Jebb, of Peterhouse, made several unsuccessful attempts to bring about an annual examination by the university of all its undergraduates; his persistent agitation is evidence of impatience with the obsolete forms which hindered progress in both universities. Knox, when proposing a similar scheme to lord North, made the proviso that examinations 'should be conducted with such delicacy as not to hurt the feelings of the diffident and modest.' Oxford's agitation for the reconstitution of the exercises for a degree was closed in 1800 by the passing of the Public Examination statute.

During the third quarter of the century, prizes for Latin essays and for Greek and Latin odes and epigrams were founded, an evidence of decline in literary arts which had long been practised in both universities. But a quite different purpose led to the foundation at Cambridge of the Townshend's prize for an English essay on an economic question (1755—6), the crown endowment of the chair of chemistry (1766), the Jacksonian professorship of 'natural and experimental philosophy' (1783) and the chair of the laws of England (1788). At Oxford, the Radcliffe observatory dates from 1777 and the Rawlinson professorship of Anglo-Saxon from 1795. It is significant of the time that the Cambridge professor of chemistry (Farish) treated his subject in its application 'to the arts and manufactures of Britain,' 'a new and useful field of instruction'; his prospectus of lectures for 1793 is a miscellaneous programme of applied science in general. Unofficial teachers then resident in Cambridge offered opportunity for the study of modern languages. William Gooch, second wrangler in 1791, who sailed in that year for the Pacific on a boundaries' commission, proposed to take with him not only mathematical books, but also works in Latin, Greek, French, Italian and Spanish; he learned the last from Isola, Gray's tutor in Italian.

During the second half of the eighteenth century, nonconformist academies[2] decreased in number, and the attempt to make them places of general education, released from particular denominational or professional ties, did not succeed. Some of their teachers were men of distinguished attainments, of whom Joseph Priestley, in early life a tutor in the Warrington academy, was the greatest and most versatile. Their readiness to experiment with

---

[1] Ingram, R. A., *The necessity of introducing divinity,*' etc. (1792); *Remarks upon the enormous expense,* etc. (1783).

[2] See *Cambridge History of English Literature,* vol. IX, pp. 392—5, and vol. X, pp. 381—3.

new courses of study was even more pronounced than it had been a century earlier. But, at a time when, in spite of ancient prestige and material advantages, the universities failed to inspire public confidence, the new institutions suffered from disabilities of their own. Their teachers were too few to treat efficiently the wide range of studies attempted, and students were seldom able enough to digest an encyclopaedic curriculum. In consequence, there was a toleration of the superficial which may have contributed to prevent the academies from becoming instruments of university reform ; and their acceptance of the position of theological seminaries for the training of ministers, a position which they had always partially occupied, removed them finally from the main current of national education. Nevertheless, they had done good service in the cause of history, literature and modern studies, particularly in respect of science and those forms of knowledge which are immediately applicable to the affairs of daily life[1]. Thomas Barnes, afterwards principal of the Manchester academy, with the support of the newly established Literary and Philosophical society of that town founded (1783) a college of Arts and Science, which anticipated, in a humble way, the scientific and technical work of modern universities and university colleges[2].

At the public schools, the studies and the method of education remained in substance the same as they were in the period 1660—1760[3]. The interesting point in their history is the prominent social place now assumed for the first time by Harrow, under a succession (1760—1805) of former Eton masters, Sumner, Heath and Drury, and by Rugby under another Etonian, Thomas James (1778—94). The number of boys in residence fluctuated considerably during the second half of the eighteenth century, and in some schools that number, at the close of the century, was very much less than it had been at the beginning. Westminster, Winchester and, in particular, Shrewsbury, are cases in point. Cowper's incomplete and prejudiced picture of the public school, which he drew in *Tirocinium*, was less true in the year 1785, when the poem appeared, than in his own school-days (1741—9); but the character of turbulence ascribed by the poet to public school education was well deserved at both the later and the earlier period. The stock question addressed by George III to Etonians whom he chanced to meet—

---

[1] See Priestley's *Miscellaneous Observations* (1778).

[2] Thompson, J., *The Owens College* (1886), introductory chapter.

[3] See *Camb. Hist. Eng. Lit.*, vol. IX, pp. 408 ff. See also p. 8 below.

'Have you had any rebellions lately, eh? eh?'—might have been put quite as aptly to any public school boy of the time. From 1770, when the Riot act was read to the Wykehamists, down to 1832, when Keate suppressed his last rebellion at Eton, there was a constant recurrence of these outbreaks; insubordination was met by arbitrary measures that seem to show an ignorance or wilful disregard of boy-nature, which in itself gives a partial explanation of the boys' unruliness. But, rough as public school life confessedly then was, it was not wanting in gentler elements. At Eton, a small editorial committee, of which John Hookham Frere was a member, produced, in 1786, *The Microcosm*, modelled on the periodical essays and miscellanies in which the time was prolific. The rival school, Westminster, had its *Trifler* in 1788, to which Robert Southey, then in the school, made a rejected contribution; his management of his own magazine, *The Flagellant*, led to his expulsion. Like most of their kind, of which they were the first, these school miscellanies were ephemeral.

Of the education of girls above the purely elementary stage, it is unnecessary to add to the account already given of its condition during the first half of the eighteenth century[1], except, perhaps, to say that its imperfections had become more obvious to contemporary critics, and that some steps had been taken to amend them, as Sir Anthony Absolute and Mrs Malaprop indirectly testify.

'We have *young ladies ... boarded and educated*,' says Miss Alscrip (in Burgoyne's *The Heiress*, 1786), 'upon blue boards in gold letters in every village, with a strolling player for dancing master, and a deserter from Dunkirk to teach the French grammar.'

The mother-tongue and drawing were regarded as studies especially appropriate to girls, and by the end of the century botany had been placed in the same category. The opinion was fairly general that girls and young women of all but the highest social standing, or great wealth, ought to receive instruction of a distinctly 'useful' domestic kind, with small regard to its formative value[2]; the others were to acquire 'accomplishments' for the purpose of ornament and to occupy time which would otherwise certainly be spent in mischief. This ideal of the socially distinguished had great attraction for those who lacked both time and means to realise it in any appreciable degree, and the consequence was that, throughout the first half of the nineteenth century, the pursuit

---

[1] See *Camb. Hist. of Eng. Lit.*, vol. IX, pp. 401—4.

[2] Adam Smith unreservedly praises the current manner of educating girls on this very ground.

of 'accomplishments,' as such, reacted injuriously upon the instruction of girls and women generally. A work on education long very popular in France and England, *Adèle et Théodore* (1782), by Madame de Genlis, bluntly asserted that women 'are born to a life both monotonous and dependent.... In their case, genius is a useless and dangerous endowment, which takes them out of their natural state.' So long as this judgment reflected public opinion, a superficial education for girls was more than tolerated. Only a revolutionary like Mary Wollstonecraft could plead that sex alone should not determine the course of study, and that schoolboys and schoolgirls should be educated together.

The aims and methods of schools of good, but not of the first, standing, may be inferred from Knox's *Liberal Education*. The author, who was master of Tunbridge school from 1778 to 1812, and a very popular writer for some forty years, was always a staunch upholder of 'the established manner' in education. The basis of all sound instruction was to be found in Latin and Greek alone ; but, when the foundation had been laid, it was desirable to include modern studies in the superstructure. The school was primarily concerned with the grammar of the two languages and the writing of verse and of prose in both ; the list of authors to be read was but a short one. To these indispensable studies there might be added, as opportunity offered, the elements of geography and history, French, some mathematics and such accomplishments as music, drawing and fencing. These last received only a tepid encouragement from Knox, who was more warmly in favour of dancing and 'the learning of the military exercise, which is now very common.' Boys were expected to read English and easy Latin books in their leisure time ; it was a general rule of practice with Knox that as much self-initiated effort as possible should be exacted from the pupil. He set his face against all such debilitating aids as translations, 'keys,' 'introductions' and the like.

That the established curriculum was not universally satisfactory is evident from the pains Knox took to show the inadequacy of the instruction given in many private schools, commonly termed 'academies,' which prepared boys for 'business' and 'the office.' Though these academies professed to teach many things, of which Latin or, more frequently, French was one, Knox asserted that their success was confined to reading, writing and summing. Forty years later he repeated this opinion ; but the public demand in the interval had brought about a great increase in the number and efficiency of schools of this kind, the monopoly of the grammar school and the severely classical course being seriously impaired in consequence.

Carlisle (*Endowed Grammar Schools*, 1818) records the foundation of twenty-eight schools between 1700 and 1798, of which only six belong to the later half of the period ; at least one-fourth of these twenty-eight schools, in spite of their name, confined their instruction to English reading, writing and summing. In one or two cases, the endowment was expressly said to be for the benefit of girls as well as boys. The charity schools, which, at the beginning of the century, had promised to develop into a widespread system of popular schools, ceased before the accession of George III to increase in number, and those that survived had outlived their usefulness. Sarah Trimmer (*Reflections upon ... charity schools*, 1792), a critic not entirely unfriendly, describes them as teaching by rote religious formularies greatly beyond the capacity of children, while many of the teachers were incompetent to do better, and the whole plan of instruction was too sedentary.

The primary purpose of the Sunday schools started in 1780 by Thomas Stock, a Gloucester clergyman, and Robert Raikes, a newspaper proprietor of the same city, was the religious and moral instruction of the poor ; all these schools taught reading, some taught writing also and a few added to these arts simple arithmetic or 'accounts.' During the early nineteenth century, writers on public education invariably include Sunday schools and their very numerous pupils as part of the national equipment in education. These schools outdid the rapid success of the charity schools ; so early as 1784, Wesley reported that he found them springing up wherever he went. In the following year, their organisation was assured by the creation of the Sunday Schools' Union. The teachers were not all volunteers ; in some instances, where there were eighteen children in a school, the teacher was paid as many pence for his day's work, and a penny a day was deducted, or added, for each pupil less, or more, than the normal eighteen. This was done deliberately in order to induce teachers 'to be more careful about the attendance of the scholars'; it was one of two, or three, devices employed in the early Sunday schools which were adopted by the government in respect of elementary day-schools at a later time.

For those who could pay a few pence weekly, there were, by the close of the eighteenth century, an unknown number of privately conducted schools which taught reading, writing and summing, either in the evening or day-time; and many men and women followed the ancient practice of supplementing their domestic employment by teaching children. Mrs Trimmer and Joseph Lancaster (who began life as the master and proprietor of a school for the poor) both drew unfavourable pictures of the instruction given under these conditions; but their statements imply that the instruction itself was widely desired by the poor themselves and accessible even in villages[1]. For the benefit of an even humbler rank, 'schools of industry' gave instruction, for the most part to girls, in spinning, knitting and plain needlework, and to a smaller number of boys in weaving, gardening and minor handicrafts; in some cases, manual exercises were supplemented by the teaching of reading and writing. Mrs Trimmer and Hannah More were conspicuous in organising and conducting this voluntary extension of casual and strictly local efforts, sometimes supported from the parish rates, which, from the sixteenth century onwards, had been made on behalf of pauper children[2]. The inception of the 'school of industry' seems to have been due to a most retiring, public-spirited woman, Mrs E. Denward, of Hardres court, Canterbury, who, about the year 1786, induced Mrs Trimmer to put the idea of such a school into practice. In method and intention, these English schools may be compared with the experiment in educating the very poor which Pestalozzi began at Neuhof some twelve years earlier.

The disproportionate attention accorded to some features of Chesterfield's *Letters to his Son*[3] has deprived their author of his undoubted right to be ranked among the educational reformers of his time. He illustrates very fully the aristocratic prejudice against schools and universities in favour of the courtly training given by private tutors and foreign academies. But, in this respect, he is a survival from an earlier generation; boys of Chesterfield's rank who were intended, like his son, to pursue a public career swelled the revived prosperity of Eton and built up the fortunes of Harrow, in the generation which immediately followed. As an educator, Chesterfield is most emphatically a humanist. The fundamental study recommended to his son is that of his fellow-men, particularly as they exist in courts and

---

[1] See, especially, Trimmer, S., *The Oeconomy of Charity* (1801), pp. 182—3, Lancaster, J., *Improvements in Education* (1803), pp. 1—21.

[2] See *Camb. Hist. of Eng. Lit.*, vol. ix, pp. 405—6.   [3] See *op. cit.*, vol. x, chap. xi.

capital cities; protracted residence abroad, and the knowledge of languages and literatures are merely auxiliary to this study, or to rhetoric, the instrument by which men are to be persuaded or cajoled. But the humanism of Chesterfield is chiefly concerned with the humanity of his own day, with its purposes and institutions of all kinds. It is this which causes him to anticipate the changes which were completed in French and German schools before the century ended. He craves 'a pretty large circle of knowledge,' which shall include not only Latin and Greek, but, also, the spoken tongues and some of the classical books of England, France, Italy and Germany, modern history and geography, jurisprudence, with a knowledge of logic, mathematics and experimental science. Much of this learning is to be acquired through intercourse rather than through books; manners, which are of the first importance, can only be learned in the same school, with assistance from those exercises of the academy which train the body to health and grace. Much of this 'large circle' is avowedly superficial. Chesterfield feels no scruple on that account, if only his pupil can command the power of the orator to influence men[1]. From the outset of the *Letters*, the study of rhetoric is insisted upon; style is wellnigh everything, matter is of less importance. The *Letters* to A. C. Stanhope (which are more instructive and much more entertaining than those to Stanhope's son, Chesterfield's successor in the title) drop this insistence upon the cultivation of oratory; but the character of the up-bringing there recommended is much the same as that prescribed in the earlier series of letters.

Lord Kames's *Loose Hints upon Education* (1781) perfectly justifies its title. Its main topic is 'the culture of the heart,' a topic characteristic of its time, treated according to 'the system of nature.' But, in spite of the author's admiration of *Émile*, this does not mean the system of Rousseau, for its corner-stone is parental authority, and Rousseau's proposal to employ natural consequences as a moral discipline is dismissed as 'smoke.'

The eighteenth century exhibits no more sincere exponents of Locke's educational ideas than the Edgeworths of Edgeworthstown, who, for three generations, laboured persistently to apply

---

[1] Sheridan, Thos., *British Education* (1756), p. xiii, refers to Chesterfield's unrealised proposal, made while lord lieutenant of Ireland (1745—6) 'to the provost and fellows of the university for the endowment of proper lectures and exercises in the art of reading and speaking English.'

those ideas to practice within the limits of a large family. The literary monuments of their activity are the work of Richard Lovell Edgeworth and his daughter, Maria[1]; but the initial movements were due to Richard's mother, Jane (Lovell).

She had read everything that had been written on the subject of education and preferred with sound judgment the opinions of Locke; to these, with modifications suggested by her own good sense, she steadily adhered[2].

Edgeworth's own education, obtained partly in Ireland, partly in England, was very desultory; but its most effective elements owed very much more to his temperament, genius and casual opportunities than to school or university. He married the first of his four wives before he was one-and-twenty; his first child was born two years after the publication (1762) of Rousseau's *Émile*. Between the ages of three and eight, this son was brought up on Rousseau's 'system,' with results which did not entirely satisfy the father, whose subsequent experience taught him to recognise the fundamental weaknesses of Rousseau as a guide to conduct and learning. It was at this time that Edgeworth's college friend, Thomas Day (in later years author of *Sandford and Merton*) was superintending, at the age of twenty-one, the education of two orphan girls with the purpose of marrying one of them, leaving the result to decide which; he married neither. The express function of domestic educator which Edgeworth assumed from the beginning of his married life he continued so long as he lived; his last marriage was contracted at the age of fifty-four, and the number of his children was eighteen. His daughter, Maria, described him as a teacher at once patient, candid and stimulating, with a sympathetic understanding of his children and skill in adapting instruction to their individual needs : qualities hardly to be expected from his keen, vivacious temperament. But his interest in education was by no means confined to the family circle. He read widely on the subject, and, in his later years, paid special attention to the educational institutions of France; at Paris, in 1803, he met 'a German, Pestalozzi ... much celebrated on the Continent,' who 'made anatomy a principal object in his system of education'—one more illustration of Pestalozzi's difficulty in making his ideas understood. Edgeworth proposed (1809) a scheme of 'secondary' schools (the word is his) to be established throughout the country under the management of a private association; the proposal, no doubt, was suggested by a similar but much more extensive plan for popular instruction described

[1] See *Camb. Hist. Eng. Lit.*, vol. XI, chap. XIII.   [2] Edgeworth, R. L., *Memoirs*, p. 66.

in Joseph Lancaster's *Improvements in Education* (1803). One of the latest measures of the Irish parliament before the Union was a bill for the improvement of Irish education introduced by Edgeworth, who became an active member of the royal commission which subsequently enquired into the state of Irish education (1806—12).

Edgeworth's second wife, Honora Sneyd (who was married in 1773 and died in 1780) would seem to have determined the main lines upon which the Edgeworth theory of education was shaped. She and her husband wrote for their children a small book, *Harry and Lucy* (1778), which, undertaken as a supplement to Mrs Barbauld's writings, itself became the originator of *Sandford and Merton*[1], the work of their friend, Day, begun with the intention of assisting their scheme of domestic instruction. Honora Edgeworth 'was of opinion that the art of education should be considered as an experimental science ' and, to give effect to that opinion, in 1776 began to keep a register of observations concerning children, upon which her husband was still engaged nearly twenty years after her death. That record guided Maria Edgeworth in writing the collection of tales for children which she called *The Parent's Assistant* (1796); it formed the basis of fact beneath the theory applied in *Practical Education* (1798), the joint work of herself and her father and the most considerable book on its subject produced in England between John Locke and Herbert Spencer.

Practical Education derives its essential principles from Locke and from the experiential psychology expounded by Hartley and Reid; Rousseau's *Émile* is used with discrimination. It attaches the highest importance to the training of character and to the cultivation of the understanding; to effect the latter, the educator must persistently suggest to the pupil motives for acquiring knowledge. The leading theme is, of course, domestic education; in relation to the education given at a public school (which is regarded as almost exclusively a place of instruction in the two classical languages) the indispensable business of the home is to lay a firm foundation of habit and moral principles, without which the subsequent schooling is in danger of proving mischievous. True to its origin, the book makes utility the arbiter in the choice of studies and strongly urges the claims of hand-work and of

---

[1] See *Camb. Hist. Eng. Lit.*, vol. xi, p. 382. The quasi-narrative form, by which Rousseau's *Émile* (1762) tried to soften the asperities of educational theory, had many popular imitators, French and English.

positive knowledge, particularly that of natural phenomena, to inclusion in the curriculum. The reiterated recommendation of play and of spontaneous activity in general as agents of instruction is an anticipation of Froebel, without a trace of the German's mysticism. Edgeworth's own tastes and inventive skill were naturally imitated by some of his children, and his sympathetic knowledge of the experimental science taught by Franklin and Priestley inevitably brought similar studies into the domestic school-room. Notwithstanding these marks of the innovator, Edgeworth is no revolutionary in reference to the long-established rhetorical instruction of the schools. He regards as very necessary the writing and, above all, the public speaking of good English, the practice of which he would make habitual from childhood. In *Professional Education* (1809), he lays it down that the making of verses is waste of time and the writing of Latin prose is not necessary for any but the professed Latinist; yet, he considers 'a knowledge and a taste for classical literature' 'indispensably necessary to every Briton who aspires to distinction in public life, for in this country a statesman must be an orator.' As evidence of the care bestowed by Edgeworth on teaching the rudiments of English to children, it may be noted that he devised (and published in *A Rational Primer*) a set of diacritical marks which virtually make our alphabet phonetic; his ideas concerning the teaching of grammar, vernacular or foreign, and his sense of the importance of modern languages bring him abreast of the best modern practice. Yet, he and his daughter shared a common prejudice of their time against fairy-tales for children. Maria's stories in *The Parent's Assistant* were written as substitutes for those classics of the nursery, which father and daughter thought 'are not now much read'—a dismal judgment which was confirmed by Wordsworth in *The Prelude*[1].

Professional Education is the work of Edgeworth alone. Its title notwithstanding, it has very little to say respecting purely technical instruction, whether clerical, military, medical or legal. The main theme is the nature of the general, preparatory instruction which a boy should receive with a view to his life's work: a purpose which, in the author's opinion, universities and public schools ignored. The plan of the book appropriately includes a consideration of the education proper to the professions of country gentleman, statesman, prince. If the book were written today, its title would probably be 'Vocational Education.' Sydney Smith

[1] See *op. cit.*, vol. XI, chap. XVI.

made it the occasion of an *Edinburgh* review (1809), in which he condemned the excessive amount of time devoted in English education to Latin and Greek and more particularly to Latin verse-making, with a consequent impoverishment of knowledge amongst Englishmen in general.

Edgeworth represents the best of the many system-makers who tried to give effect to the principles of *Émile*. Wordsworth, although as ready as Rousseau to rely upon liberty and childish instinct as guideposts for the educator, poured scorn upon system-mongers and their product, 'the model child,' a prodigy of useful information, precocious criticism and self-conceit. *The Prelude* relates the course of the poet's own upbringing at school (1778—86) and at Cambridge (1787—91), and parenthetically shows how he himself would educate 'according to Nature'; but he is, perhaps, too prone to see the general in the particular, and, consequently, to overlook the powers and the needs of commonplace boys and men. A different note is struck in *The Excursion* (1814), the eighth and ninth books of which expose the essential evils of the industrial revolution, and express the poet's confident belief that a national scheme of education following the proposals of Andrew Bell could yet overcome them. Thirty years later, he recorded his sorrow that no such plan had been put into operation.

Maria Edgeworth's earliest book, *Letters for Literary Ladies* (1795), presents the then customary arguments on female disability as conceived by the complacent male, who is allowed, on the whole, to get the better of the dispute; incidental reference is made to the increasing attention then being paid to the education of girls. The modern touch is not wanting; a good cook, we are told, is only an empirical chemist.

An unmerited neglect has befallen the educational writings of the Edgeworths, who anticipated by nearly sixty years the introduction (1854) into England of the principles of Froebel. The Kindergarten has become the earliest form of schooling of great numbers of English children, while the Irish writers have been ignored. Yet in wisdom they exceeded most reformers, holding that

In education, we must, however, consider the actual state of manners in that world in which our pupils are to live, as well as our wishes or our hopes of its gradual improvement.

Joseph Priestley's *Miscellaneous Observations relating to Education* (1778) contains an anticipation of the first chapter of Herbert Spencer's *Education* so close in thought and phrase as to suggest Spencer's familiarity with the book. The theme is education as preparatory to 'subsistence,' and the study of natural science is the means proposed. Priestley urges a claim for a type of instruction suitable to those whose destination is neither the university nor the counting-house. Like many of his contemporaries, he believed that, if the customary curriculum was to escape general repudiation, useful knowledge must be included in it; but he was even more anxious to base a liberal education upon a course of modern studies.

No subject had greater interest for the reformers than the mother-tongue, whose educational value had been persistently asserted in England for more than a century past. But, while its indispensable place in a satisfactory curriculum might be granted, considerable doubt existed as to the best manner of teaching the vernacular, when admitted. Locke (*Some Thoughts concerning Education*) had formulated an excellent method of rudimentary instruction in English; but the difficulty of systematising the language for the purpose of tuition had not disappeared. The fluctuation of spelling and of idiom, and the absence of any generally accepted manual of grammar, were the points to which reformers addressed themselves. Swift (*A Letter to the Lord High Treasurer*)[1] had expressed the belief that it was desirable and possible to 'ascertain,' and then 'fix' the language for ever, the standard being sought in the English of Elizabeth, James and Charles; his pamphlet long survived in the memory of would-be innovators though the standard itself was shifted. A serious attempt to grapple with the asserted instability of the mother-tongue may be dated from the publication of Johnson's *Dictionary* (1755)[2], which was followed by other works intended to attain similar ends. Joseph Priestley's *Rudiments of English Grammar* (1761), originally intended as a school-book, is marked by a common-sense parsimony of technical terms very unusual in writers on the subject, and by a deference to customary usage which would shock the pedant. Robert Lowth, in his anonymously published *A Short Introduction to English Grammar* (1762), asserted that the ungrammatical English of 'polite' conversation, and of such of 'our most approved authors' as Dryden, Addison, Pope and Swift himself, was due to sheer carelessness and not to any inherent defect in the language. The method of Lowth's book

---

[1] 'A proposal for correcting, improving and ascertaining the English Tongue in a letter to the ... Earl of Oxford' (1712).

[2] See *Camb. Hist. Eng. Lit.*, vol. x, pp. 173 ff.

was adopted and its terminology further elaborated in the *English Grammar* (1795) of Lindley Murray, who may be regarded as the originator of that formal, logic-chopping treatment of its subject which long made English grammar the least profitable of school studies. This celebrated text-book had no claim to novelty beyond a careful selection of what was thought most useful, and its presentation in different sizes of printer's types in order to indicate degrees of importance. Its success was immediate and extraordinary. In the year of its author's death (1826), it had reached its fortieth edition, and, in spite of abridgments in many editions and innumerable imitations in Great Britain and America, it was still being printed in 1877. Its immediate success testifies to the great and increasing number of schools, chiefly private boarding schools, which, at the opening of the nineteenth century, made an 'English education' their avowed aim.

Thomas Sheridan, godson of Swift and father of Richard Brinsley Sheridan, published, in 1756, *British Education*, a tiresome, long-winded work, stuffed with quotations chiefly from Locke and Milton, in which he called for the standardising of English spelling, pronunciation, diction and idiom, and advocated the study of English rhetoric, the encouragement of public speaking and of the art of reading. He appeared to believe that due attention to these matters would effect the political, religious, moral and aesthetic redemption of society. Yet, in spite of his sympathy with the chief aim of the Académie Française, he would not secure these advantages by means of any academy or society, but trusted to the introduction of rhetoric and elocution into the ordinary school and college course, and, thereafter, to the critical discussion which that introduction would bring about. Sheridan proposed to give effect to his ideas by establishing a school for the post-collegiate instruction of the well-to-do on lines which, today, would be termed 'vocational'; that is, the studies pursued were to bear directly upon the future occupation of the pupil. In proposing provision upon liberal lines for the education of the future legislator, country gentleman, soldier and merchant, Sheridan was continuing the tradition of that 'doctrine of courtesy' which had added a multitude of books to European languages during some two-and-a-half centuries; and these works had always upheld the claims of vernacular languages in schemes of education. A body of very influential persons founded the Hibernian society at Dublin in 1758 with the intention of carrying out Sheridan's plan; but the project was attacked by private schoolmasters as a mere pretext for bestowing a salaried office upon its originator. Incidentally, these attacks show that there was a great deal of professional as well as public sympathy with the advocates of a modern curriculum, and some success in employing it where schools were unfettered by ancient statute. One of the assailants, the anonymous writer of *A letter to a schoolmaster in the country* (1758), wields an ironic pen reminiscent of Swift; he doubts the feasibility of giving to those who have passed through the established course of education

the air and turn of the high-rank people, as they want for a ground-work the inanity of thought and unconnected succession of ideas which make the specific difference between a gentleman and a pedant.

The scheme for a school or college propounded to the Hibernian society in 1758, and similar schemes of 1769 and 1783—4, came to nothing; but Sheridan, till the last, continued to plead for the study of rhetoric and the practice of elocution. He was one of the earliest students of English prosody[1], phonetics and spelling-reform; by insisting that language is primarily and essentially a thing spoken, not written, he anticipated the principle underlying recent changes in language-teaching.

The beginning of 'the Scottish school of rhetoric' was almost contemporary with the labours of Sheridan and Priestley. The earliest utterances of this school are to be found in the *Essays* (1742 and 1758) of David Hume, but its earliest separate publication was *Elements of Rhetoric* (1762) by Henry Home, lord Kames. From 1759 onwards, Hugh Blair lectured on 'composition' in Edinburgh with such success that a chair of rhetoric and *belles lettres* was founded for him there in 1762. The professorial discourses delivered during his occupancy of this chair were published in the year of his retirement as *Lectures on Rhetoric and Belles Lettres* (1783). The mark of this Scottish school is the attempt, not uniformly successful, to elaborate from the associational psychology[2] of the time a doctrine of taste and rules for its expression in the arts, particularly in the art of composition. The psychology and the rules and doctrine professedly deduced from it wear a detached air in the writings of Blair and Kames; in spite of their repudiation of great names and their desire to build empirically, none of the school shakes himself quite free from Aristotle and the great literary critics. But they did good service in a period greatly inclined to an exclusive rationalism

[1] See, *op. cit.*, vol. xi, pp. 250, 255.   [2] See, *op. cit.*, vol. x, p. 342.

by asserting the fundamental nature of emotion and its necessary part in the production and enjoyment of all forms of art; their pupils were prepared to welcome wholeheartedly the literary principles of Wordsworth, Byron and Scott. George Campbell's *The Philosophy of Rhetoric*, begun in 1750 and published in 1776, succeeds best in presenting its theme systematically and without much embarrassment from its psychological groundwork; Campbell remains to this day a helpful critic of diction, though he is sometimes meticulous in cases where his own sound criterion of 'reputable use' is against him. Blair's three-volume *Lectures* is a magazine for reference rather than an ordered system of instruction; as tutorial work to be used in large classes, the lectures may have proved interesting and useful to attentive students, but, as a book, they are very tedious. The third volume presents in germ the general idea of literature distinguishable from its various national varieties. A secondary feature in the teaching of the Scottish school is the great importance which it attributed to the arts of public reading and speaking. In the distinct course of study proposed by Knox (*Liberal Education*, 1781), he included these accomplishments, on the ground that English ought to form a great part of an English gentleman's education. Enfield's *The Speaker* (1774) quickly established itself in common use and long retained its vogue as an authoritative anthology of 'recitations' from Shakespeare, Sterne, Pope and more modern writers; its author, who was a tutor at the Warrington academy after Priestley's time, expressly intended his book to be associated with the Scottish teaching of rhetoric. Its early success points to a considerable number of schools and schoolmasters in sympathy with some recognition of the vernacular as an educational instrument.

The psychology of Locke and its educational corollaries[1] were fully appreciated and further developed in France, where, by 1793, they became co-ordinated in the demand for a state-maintained system of schools, primary and secondary, with additional provision for higher and professional education, the primary stage of this system at least being gratuitous and universally obligatory. In England, the desire to see a great increase in the means of popular instruction of some sort was fairly general amongst thinking men; but there was much hesitation in determining the part to be played by the state itself in the matter. As early as 1756, Thomas Sheridan in *British Education*

[1] See, *op. cit.*, vol. IX, p. 401.

had asserted that 'in every State it should be a fundamental
maxim that the education of youth should be particularly formed
and adapted to the nature and end of its government'—a principle
which John Brown made more explicit by a proposal for universal
instruction imposed by law with a view to instilling 'the manners
and principles on which alone the State can rest[1].' The last word
is significant; for Brown and Sheridan alike, the state was an
entity to which change could only be fatal. The danger attending
that opinion was exposed by Joseph Priestley (*An essay on the
first principles of government,* 1768), who reminded Brown and
other admirers of Spartan officialism that 'uniformity is the
characteristic of the brute creation.'

Education is a branch of civil liberty which ought by no means to be sur-
rendered into the hands of a civil magistrate, and the best interests of
society require that the right of conducting it be inviolably preserved to
individuals.

The prominent position as public teacher, educational reformer,
man of science and political thinker to which Priestley attained
in later years gave an authority to this opinion which more than
counterbalanced the rambling diffuseness of Sheridan and the
industrious pamphleteering of Brown. It became an accepted
article of the radical creed that, in the interest of liberty, the
state's intervention in public education should be reduced as
much as possible; in consequence, the history of English educational administration between 1790 and 1870 marks a very slow
movement from private, cooperative activity to public control
grudgingly admitted. In her own day, Mary Wollstonecraft (*A
Vindication of the Rights of Woman,* 1792) stood almost alone
in her readiness to accept the French conception in full. The
prevalent opinion was better expressed by William Godwin
(*Enquiry concerning political justice,* etc., 1796): 'the project
of national education ought uniformly to be discouraged on
account of its obvious alliance with national government.' But
Godwin's doctrine, as expressed in this work, is the negation of
all social cooperation; and the desire to extend instruction to
the great bulk of the people, when confronted with the problem
of its cost, in the end compelled the unwilling to accept state
support. For two centuries before the appearance of *The Wealth
of Nations* (1776), Scotsmen had been familiar with the idea of
public education supported by public funds, and, since 1696, they
had been putting the idea into practice. It is, therefore, not

---

[1] *Thoughts on Civil Liberty* (1765), p. 591.

surprising to discover Adam Smith laying it down that a man uneducated is a man mutilated and that, since an ignorant person is an element of weakness in the community, public education is a mode of national defence. Nevertheless, he thinks that the state's part should be limited to making elementary instruction compulsory and to supplying the money required to meet any deficiency in voluntary contributions; the absence of competition, from which public and endowed institutions like universities and grammar schools suffer, leads unavoidably to inefficiency and neglect. Instruction should be almost self-supporting. Still, the state might impose an examination-test 'even in the higher and more difficult sciences' upon all candidates for professional employment, and an examination in reading, writing and reckoning should be passed before a man could become a freeman, or set up a trade in a corporate town or village. Thomas Paine (*The Rights of Man*, 1791) believed that 'a nation under a well-regulated government should permit none to remain uninstructed'; but he would not have the state establish or directly maintain schools. Paine endeavoured to make these opinions harmonise by suggesting that grants, or remission of taxes, should be allowed in respect of individual children, on condition that the parents made a payment for their instruction. Like Adam Smith, he saw no difficulty in finding teachers : 'there are always persons of both sexes to be found in every village, especially when growing into years, capable of such an undertaking.' Events proved that the magnitude of the task was vastly underrrated.

The subject passed beyond the range of merely academic discussion on the appearance of Joseph Lancaster's *Improvements in Education* (1803). Apart from its account of the author's mode of organising a school, 'the monitorial or mutual system,' a device for which he was greatly indebted to Andrew Bell[1], the chief merit of this pamphlet lies in its scheme for making elementary instruction general. Lancaster believed that the matter was one of 'national concern,' which sectarianism alone had hindered from coming by its own ; but he was equally against the enactment of a 'compulsive law,' applied either to schoolchildren or their teachers. He proposed the establishment of a voluntary society 'on general Christian principles' (that is, destitute of denominational associations), having as its objects 'the promotion of good morals and the instruction of youth in useful learning adapted to their respective situations.' These

---

[1] *Experiments in Education* (1798, 2nd edn, 1805).

objects were to be attained by the bestowal of the society's patronage upon masters and mistresses already at work in their own schools who proved worthy of encouragement, by offering prizes to school-children for regular and punctual attendance, by establishing schools (this was inserted with some hesitation), by setting up a public library containing books on education for the information of teachers, by enabling teachers to obtain school material at cost price and by instituting a teachers' friendly society. Lancaster assumed that the aims of his proposed association could be achieved 'in some hundreds of schools amongst many thousands of children at an expence that probably would not exceed £1500 *per annum.*'

Lancaster's suggestion that his proposed society should rest upon an undenominational basis roused the opposition of Sarah Trimmer, who had become obsessed by the notion that a conspiracy against Christianity, originally contrived, as she conceived, by the French Encyclopedists, was threatening these islands. To defeat this plot, she had established *The Guardian of Education* (1802—6), a magazine full of orthodox prejudice which is of importance to the bibliographer of education, though the book-notices of which it chiefly consists possess few other merits. Lancaster's *Improvements* was thought to deserve not only an elaborate review in this periodical, but, also, a counterblast in the form of a bulky pamphlet, *A comparative view of the New Plan of Education promulgated by Mr Joseph Lancaster* (1805). Mrs Trimmer agreed that 'an interference of the Legislature in respect to the education of the common people' was 'highly necessary.' But she declared that a national system already existed, and she entirely disapproved of societies founded on so indefinite a conception as 'general Christian principles.' Instead of adopting this conception (the appearance of which in the field of education she rightly traced to the German apostle of natural religion, J. B. Basedow (1724—90)), she would, with Priestley, leave each religious body free to instruct its children in accordance with its own tenets. The church of England was the established church, and the acts of Uniformity prescribed the study of the church catechism and the use of the Book of Common Prayer; these, therefore, constituted a national system of education, with the charity schools and grammar schools as its agents, and with the bishops in the exercise of functions that had belonged to them from time immemorial as its chief authorities. Yet Lancaster desired to replace this legally constituted system by an innovation which, notwithstanding its merit as a chief and feasible mode of organising popular schools, was ill-grounded and mischievous. John Bowles (*Letter to Whitbread*, 1807) put Mrs Trimmer's point of view succinctly: 'when education is made a national concern, youth must be brought up as members of the national church.'

The main issue thus raised took the discussion at once into the wider arena of political questions, where it secured considerable attention. Lancaster's 'undenominational' system was regarded by tories and churchmen as a deliberate attack upon the establishment; whigs and dissenters cherished it as a guarantee of religious liberty. The essential weakness of the method of instruction advocated by Bell and Lancaster, in which pupils were entirely taught by fellow-pupils, was forgotten by the critics in their anxiety to deal with an accident of 'the Mutual System,' namely, the character of the religious instruction to be imparted. Wordsworth (*The Prelude*, 1799—1805) and Coleridge (*Biographia Literaria*, 1815—17) had ridiculed methodisers and mechanical forms of teaching; but both were warm adherents of Bell. Pamphlets, reviews and sermons urged the respective merits of the 'Madras' and 'Lancasterian' 'systems,' or the claim of their respective authors to rank as 'discoverers.' Sydney Smith, Robert Owen, Henry Brougham, William Wilberforce, Romilly, Samuel Rogers and James Mill were sympathisers with, or active supporters of, Lancaster. Southey, in a *Quarterly Review* article (October 1811), vindicated against *The Edinburgh Review* (November 1810) Bell's right to be considered Lancaster's forerunner, and exposed the evils and absurdities which he held to mark Lancaster's mode of school management. The climax of the dispute was reached in a sermon preached at St Paul's in June 1811 by the Cambridge lady Margaret professor, Herbert Marsh, in which he repeated Mrs Trimmer's arguments on national education, the church and undenominationalism. The sermon was followed immediately by the formation of a committee whose labours took effect, in October 1811, in the institution of 'the National Society for promoting the education of the Poor in the principles of the Established Church.' The rival organisation was 'the British and Foreign School Society' (1814), the successor of the Royal Lancasterian institute and Lancaster's committee founded in 1808. Thus, 'the voluntary system' of English elementary schools was begun, and a compromise between state interference and individualism was effected, which lasted till 1870. The desire, fervently expressed in *The Excursion*, for a state-controlled education based on the Madras system was not realised; although many Englishmen were willing to extend a modicum of instruction to the poor as an act of grace, very few agreed with Wordsworth, Pestalozzi and Kant in regarding education as 'a sacred right' inherent in human nature.

The faults of the mutual or monitorial system are obvious; yet, contemporary opinion ranked it as a great discovery or invention, a nostrum for all the ills of education. Bell honestly believed that he was introducing no mere expedient for making a minimum of mechanical instruction accessible to large numbers, but a true educational *organon* capable of changing the whole aspect of society and applicable to all grades of instruction. Lancaster's claims were not a whit more restricted. Mutual instruction was introduced into Charterhouse (1813), where it survived in favour for at least five years; a few grammar schools and some private boarding schools followed the example. Families of wealth and position in London combined to form their own little Madras school, with 'a most charming monitor boy' from the Central school in Baldwin's Gardens to act as master. Pillans employed the plan in the High School of Edinburgh. Measures were taken to make the system known on the continent, particularly in France; and it attained a new distinction from the genius and devotion which father Girard displayed in the elementary schools of Fribourg. Jeremy Bentham (*Chrestomathia*, 1816) identified himself with an abortive scheme for founding 'The Chrestomathic [*i.e.* Useful Knowledge] Day school,' to teach a thousand boys and girls the circle of the sciences on the lines of 'the New Instruction System.'

At first, the National and British societies had no association with the state; but their contributions to national education were so many and so important that when, in 1833, parliament agreed to an annual grant of £20,000 'to be issued in aid of private subscriptions for the erection of school houses for the education of the children of the poorer classes in Great Britain,' the money was handed to the societies for allocation, on condition that at least an equal sum was privately subscribed.

The earliest attempts of Robert Owen to revolutionise society were made by way of the school. When, in 1799, he took over the New Lanark mills from David Dale, he found a plan of instruction in operation for mill-children, which had but small success, owing to the fact that it was conducted in the evening at the termination of a long day's work. By gradual elaboration, carried out between 1799 and 1816, this instruction was expanded into the New Institution for the Formation of Character, which, in its full form, included an adult evening-school, a day-school for children whose ages ranged from six to ten and an infant-school for little ones of a year old and upwards. It was an axiom of Owen that character is formed from without, not attained from within, that 'circumstances' are all-powerful in the process of its formation. The basal principles of the New Institution were that a child's mind is absolutely plastic and that human nature is innately good, two characteristic eighteenth century beliefs derived from Locke and Rousseau. The instruction given in the two schools was presented conversationally and intuitively: that is, knowledge of things was communicated not through books, but by means of the things themselves, or representations of them other than verbal. It was impressed upon each child that he 'must endeavour to make his companions happy.' The teaching included reading, writing, summing, the Bible and the Shorter catechism, history, geography, music, dancing and 'the military discipline' for both sexes. Owen claimed that his schools made children both rational and altruistic; the fame of New Lanark was widespread, and visitors, many of them distinguished, came in large numbers to inspect the social life of the place, and of its children more especially. But, by his attacks on all particular forms of religion, Owen shocked the majority of his partners in business, and, in 1824, these succeeded in destroying the peculiar character of the New Institution by bringing it within the system of the British and Foreign School society. The New Lanark experiment played a considerable part in demonstrating the value and feasibility of popular schools at a time when the subject was prominent in the public mind; its more precise result was the institution of infant-schools, whose extension throughout England was primarily due to the Infant School society (founded in 1824) and to the labours of its superintendent, Samuel Wilderspin.

The establishment of *The Edinburgh Review*[1], in 1802, brought Scottish and English education into a new and unanticipated relationship. During its early days (1807—11), the reviewers, more especially Sydney Smith and Henry Brougham, developed a policy of hostile criticism, of which English educational institutions were the object. The monopoly conferred upon Greek and Latin by grammar schools and universities, the consequent indifference to the claims of 'useful knowledge,' the futility of current modes of educating girls, were all unsparingly denounced; Lancaster was supported as a genuine apostle of popular

---

[1] See *Camb. Hist. Eng. Lit.*, vol. XII, chap. VI.

instruction, while his orthodox rivals were ridiculed. Brougham's own education was chiefly Scottish; the studies in mathematics, physics and chemistry which, while an Edinburgh undergraduate, he had followed under such distinguished *savants* and teachers as John Playfair and Joseph Black, left an indelible impression upon his sympathies and mode of thought. He was a great admirer of the Scots parish school, that unbroken channel between the veriest rudiments and the classes of 'the college.' As member of parliament, he was associated with Samuel Whitbread and others belonging to the active group which advocated popular instruction and the monitorial system. After Whitbread's death, Brougham became the parliamentary leader of this group, and, in 1816, he secured the appointment of a select committee to enquire into the education of the lower orders of the metropolis. This committee extended its enquiries to schools outside London and to schools not usually regarded as coming within the terms of their reference. The administration of educational endowments in general was impeached by the committee's report of 1818, and by Brougham's *Letter to Samuel Romilly ... upon the abuse of charities* (1818), a pamphlet which ran through ten editions within a few months. The committee's enquiry was prejudiced in origin, its chairman, Brougham, was dictatorial and its report menaced innocent as well as guilty; its inaccuracy was proved in particular cases like Winchester and Croydon[1]. Yet, the abuses denounced were notorious. Masters who had few or no free pupils, or no pupils at all, were endowed with schoolhouses and incomes; in some places, where the demand for grammar schools had died out, trustees were, in effect, misappropriating the endowments for their own benefit. Brougham and his friends were mistaken when they interpreted the phrase *pauperes et indigentes*, describing the beneficiaries of educational endowments, as though it were used in the sense conveyed by the English term 'indigent poor'; but there was reason in their contention that those endowments were not doing all that was possible for national education. A blind alley seemed to have been reached by Eldon's ruling in the chancery court (1805; reaffirmed some twenty years later), that grammar schools must employ trust funds for the teaching of Latin, Greek and Hebrew alone; to draw upon them for instruction in French, German or other modern studies would be misappropriation. But, in spite of chancery and their own statutes, a good many

---

[1] Bowles, W. L., *Vindiciae Wykehamicae*; dean Ireland, *Letter to Henry Brougham* (1819).

grammar schools, perhaps one-fourth of the total number, were being conducted as elementary or 'commercial' schools[1].

The situation, as Brougham conceived it, was that property of great value had been devised for the education of the indigent poor, but that the bequest was useless because instruction was confined to three ancient languages. The parliamentary remedy seemed plain; he brought in two bills, the first (1818) to direct a comprehensive survey of all educational charities, the second (1820) to apply the parish school system of Scotland to her southern sister. By the latter bill, it was proposed to empower grammar schools to teach reading, writing and arithmetic as well as the statutory classical tongues; elementary schools were to be built at the national expense in every parish, whose householders were to pay the schoolmaster's salary. This second bill was defeated by the dissenters, who regarded it as a measure for increasing the authority and powers of bishops and parish clergy. The bill of 1818 passed into law, but lord Liverpool's government emasculated it by confining its sphere to charities unquestionably intended to act as poor-relief. So late as 1835, lord Brougham was still advocating the principles of 1818 and 1820; but, by that time, he had satisfied himself that the 'voluntary system' was competent to satisfy the claims of national education.

The rapid increase in number, throughout Great Britain, of Mechanics' institutions confirms the statement of contemporary observers that there was a widespread desire among urban populations for instruction. They owed their beginning to an associate of the first *Edinburgh* reviewers, George Birkbeck, a fellow-student and lifelong friend of Brougham. Birkbeck, who was professor of natural philosophy at the Andersonian institution, Glasgow, from 1799 to 1804, opened, in 1800, a free course of Saturday evening lectures to artisans, intended to familiarise them with some of the scientific principles underlying the employment of tools and machinery. The class met with immediate success and survived its originator's removal to London. Under his successor, it experienced a variety of fortunes, till, in 1823, a number of seceding members established the Glasgow Mechanics' institution and made Birkbeck its president. In the meantime, he was practising medicine in London, where he had become a member of the circle which included George Grote, Jeremy Bentham, James Mill, Joseph Hume, David Ricardo, John Cam Hobhouse, Sir Francis

---

[1] See *A letter to Henry Brougham…from an M.A. of Queen's College, Oxford, upon the best method of restoring decayed grammar schools* (1818).

Burdett, Francis Place, Brougham and others whose political principles ranged them with the philosophical radicals. A suggestion made in 1823 by *The Mechanics' Magazine*, that the Glasgow example should be followed in London, was eagerly taken up by Birkbeck and his friends; the result was the creation of the London Mechanics' institution (better known today as Birkbeck college), the development of which became the lifelong preoccupation of the man whose name it now bears. Thirteen hundred members registered themselves at the outset; the course of study was chiefly scientific and practical, though it found room, also, for 'French, stenography, botany, mnemonics and phrenology.'

Brougham, with Birkbeck, one of the four original trustees of the new institution, greatly strengthened the educational policy of the group to which he and his friend belonged, by the publication, in 1825, of *Practical Observations upon the education of the people addressed to the working classes and their employers*, a pamphlet which gained as much attention as had been accorded to his *Letter to Romilly*. Here, in brief compass, the whole scheme for adult education was described. Two main lines of activity were proposed. Lectures to artisans, libraries, book clubs and 'conversation societies,' that is, tutorial classes, constituted the first; the encouragement of cheap publications and the preparation of elementary treatises on mathematics, physics and other branches of science formed the second. It was Brougham's opinion that the business of controlling Mechanics' institutions was a valuable element in the education of their members, and that the institutions themselves, once started, should and could be self-supporting. He probably overrated, in both respects, the ability of the working men of the time, as he certainly overrated the value of public lectures to persons whose preliminary instruction and training were slender. For a score of years after the foundation of the earliest of them, Mechanics' institutions increased in number and in extension over England and Scotland; but, at an early stage in their history, they ceased to be recruited in greater part from among artisans. It was this failure, added to the defective conception of education encouraged by Mechanics' institutions, which led Frederick Denison Maurice, F. J. Furnivall, Thomas Hughes, J. M. Ludlow, Charles Kingsley, John Ruskin and others to form, or support, the Working Men's college (1854), the word 'college' emphasising the close relationship between all who shared its life, either as teachers or pupils. The object of the college was to place a liberal education within the reach of working men by providing instruction in those subjects which it most concerns English citizens to know. The absence of a clearly defined purpose in the minds of the working men auditors goes far to explain the failure of Mechanics' institutions to help those for whom they were especially started. The driving force of such a purpose is illustrated by the success of the Working Men's college, the much later Ruskin college and, more especially, the University Tutorial classes of the Workers' Educational association[1].

In spite of the heavy duty on paper (threepence on the pound weight), a periodical like *The Mechanics' Magazine*, devoted to applied science and the processes of manufacture, and published weekly at threepence, secured 'an extensive circulation.' Brougham, therefore, hoped that cheapening the cost of book-production would render possible the publication of reprints of works on ethics, politics and history. This part of the scheme was realised in the publications of the Society for the Diffusion of Useful Knowledge, founded in 1827, with Brougham as its first president. The prevalence, in these works, of the principles which, about that time, came to be known as 'utilitarian,' and the omission of reference to Christian beliefs, caused them to be regarded askance by Thomas Arnold and others, whose genuine interest in the education of working people cannot be questioned. The society's publications (most of them issued by Charles Knight) included *The Penny Magazine* (1832—7), *The Penny Cyclopaedia* (1832, etc.), *The Quarterly Journal of Education* (1831—5), *The Library of Entertaining Knowledge*, *The Library of Useful Knowledge* and an uncompleted *Biographical Dictionary* (1842—4). Lord Brougham and Birkbeck took part in the movement for the abolition of the tax of fourpence a copy levied on newspapers ; the tax was reduced in 1836 to one penny, at which figure it remained till its disappearance in 1855.

Reviews of La Place's *Mécanique Celeste* (1808 ; probably by Playfair) and of Falconer's *Strabo* (1809 ; in part by Sydney Smith) gave *The Edinburgh* an occasion for attacking the universities, both of which were held responsible for the backward state of mathematical investigation in England. Cambridge made mathematics the great object of study, but, like the sister university, adhered exclusively to antiquated methods ; Oxford taught only the rudiments, 'mistaking the infancy of science for its maturity.' According to the reviewer, while the elder university

---

[1] See Mansbridge, A., *University Tutorial Classes* (1913).

possessed a richly endowed press, it published bad versions of classical texts, edited in 'Oxonian Latin,' whose 'parent language' was no other than the 'vulgar English' of the day. These reviews were followed, in 1810, by Sydney Smith's attack on the public school system of education, the charge against it being that it failed to produce men eminent in science or letters. Edward Copleston, at the moment professor of poetry, defended Oxford in three *Replies* to these 'calumnies,' in which, incidentally, he described the degree examinations and the tutorial system, which he preferred to the professorial lectures of the Scottish universities. But the defence was weak and largely irrelevant. Copleston was on fairly safe ground so long as he argued that a truer education results from the knowledge of men which is conveyed by literature, than from the knowledge of matter and motion which is derived from science. But, when the function of a university is in question, he fails to meet, or even to understand, his adversaries. He held that universities are schools for those who are to become political leaders or clergymen, and that for these classes the humanities are the most fitting instruction. The *Edinburgh* reviewers knew that there were other classes requiring advanced instruction of a kind which the literary curriculum of the English universities could not give. Copleston thought it sufficient to reply that 'miscellaneous knowledge,' as he called it, was 'esteemed and encouraged' at Oxford, though it was 'the subordinate and not the leading business of education.' A man with a well disciplined mind can attain knowledge of this kind 'after he enters into life.' This, of course, was what the critics denied ; and, if it were so, the universities were ignoring their duty of research. They were places of education, but not homes of learning or sources of that useful knowledge which the times imperatively required.

Two visits to the newly founded university of Bonn (1818), paid by Thomas Campbell in the summer and autumn of 1820, made a deep impression upon the poet. In particular, he appears to have conceived, at that time, the idea of a university for London which should reproduce the educational aims, scope and professorial organisation of the German model, with which his own Glasgow education predisposed him to sympathise. He mooted the idea among his associates, and finally made it public in a letter to *The Times* (9 February 1825), thus coming into touch with Henry Brougham and the group of thinkers who were anxious for the general diffusion of knowledge and a radical change in English educational institutions. The nonconformist bodies of

London, whose members were virtually shut out from the older universities, heartily welcomed the scheme, and they were joined by churchmen who desired to see in the metropolis a university devoted to modern studies and free from the expense entailed by residence in colleges. So marked was the adhesion of these born opponents, that Campbell feared it would be necessary to provide two theological chairs, one for church and one for dissent; but Brougham succeeded in eliminating divinity from the scheme. In February 1826, the proprietors and donors who had furnished the capital formally constituted themselves 'an institution for the general advancement of literature and science by affording young men opportunities for obtaining literary and scientific education at a moderate expense'; the institution being styled 'the University of London.' The duke of Sussex laid the foundation-stone of the building in Gower street early in 1827 and, on 2 October 1828, lectures began to some 300 students. In the meantime, the church became alarmed at the divorce between education and religion represented by the new establishment. At midsummer, 1828, the duke of Wellington, then prime minister, presided over a public meeting which resolved to found a college for general education in which, while literature and science were subjects of instruction, it should be essential that the doctrines and duties of Christianity, as inculcated by the church of England, should be taught. This second institution received its charter as King's college, London, in August 1829, and the college was opened in October 1831.

One of the gravest objections to the existing English university system made by the innovators was that it reduced the university and its accredited teachers, the professors, to impotence, and installed in their stead the colleges and the tutorial system. This objection was almost savagely urged by Sir William Hamilton in *The Edinburgh Review* (June and December 1831); were the practice reversed, the advancement of knowledge would follow and, incidentally, one serious obstacle to the admission of non-conformists to universities would be removed. In these opinions Thomas Arnold concurred. The institution of two colleges in London, therefore, infringed an essential principle of the scheme introduced by admirers of the Scottish and German organisation of university teaching. The same disregard of this principle was shown in the foundation of the university of Durham in 1832.

Of the two London colleges, the earlier did not succeed in securing a charter, though, in 1831, it came very near doing so.

Both colleges were impeded by the partisan squabbles which were inevitable in consequence of their origin ; but a workable agreement was reached by the ministry of Sir Robert Peel in November 1836. On the same day, the elder college received its charter under the style 'University College, London' and a new corporation was created—

persons eminent in literature and science to act as a board of examiners and to perform all the functions of the examiners in the Senate house of Cambridge; this body to be termed 'The University of London.'

Students of the two colleges alone were at first admissible to these examinations ; but the qualification was, in 1850, extended to a number of affiliated colleges in different parts of the country, the result proving so unsatisfactory that, in 1858, the restriction of affiliation was removed altogether, while it was laid down that (with the exception of certain medical requirements) all degrees and distinctions were to be obtained solely by proficiency shown in the examinations of the university. In other words, its work, henceforth, was confined to examining, a function whose importance was unduly exaggerated in consequence; the link with the two chief London colleges was, in effect, broken, and the possibility of bringing order and system into the higher education of London was postponed for some forty years.

Hamilton's dislike of the tutorial system and the exaggerated reverence for German educational institutions, which he and Campbell did much to propagate, blinded him to the merits of moderate reforms proposed by such men as William Whewell. In *Thoughts on the Study of Mathematics* (1835), Whewell had contrasted 'philosophy' taught by lectures with mathematics taught tutorially, and had asserted that the latter was by far the more efficient instrument of education ; but the advantage was lost, if the teaching were too abstract and dissociated from 'that great system of physical knowledge ... with the character and nature of which no liberally educated man ought to be unacquainted.' He suggested that mechanics and hydrostatics should be included in every examination for the B.A. degree. Hamilton's review[1] was a tiresome piece of pedantry and bad writing, which ignored Whewell's agreement with the contention of the earlier reviewers. The Cambridge tutor turned the tables upon him very happily[2], and the subsequent history of German universities in their adoption of laboratory and tutorial methods fully justified the position taken by Whewell.

---

[1] *The Edinburgh Review* (June 1836)
[2] *On the principles of English university education* (1837).

Popular tradition, supported by Stanley's *Life* (1844) and Hughes's *Tom Brown's School Days* (1857), regards Thomas Arnold as the universal reformer or re-creator of public schools. But, so far as the purely professional side of school-keeping is concerned, he was anticipated by Samuel Butler, headmaster of Shrewsbury from 1798 to 1836, of which period only the last eight years fall within Arnold's tenure of office at Rugby (1828—42). The decline from which public schools had suffered was nowhere more evident than at Shrewsbury, where, in 1798, there were not more than twenty boys. Assisted by a reconstituted governing body, Butler built upon this remnant a flourishing school, whose achievements and organisation became models for Eton and Harrow, as Hawtrey headmaster of Eton from 1834 to 1853, generously acknowledged to Butler himself. Periodical examinations, and a carefully super-vised scheme of 'marks' assigned for merit and industry, sustained an emulation that gave new life to the studies of Shrewsbury boys, which was manifested in their extraordinary successes in competi-tion for university scholarships. The responsibility thrown upon 'preposters'—'the eight boys to whom the master delegates a certain share of authority'—revived an ancient usage whose in-vention is often ascribed to Arnold alone. The importance which Butler attached to 'private work,' study done in the boys' leisure time and under no supervision, was part of his unwavering policy of training his pupils to initiative and self-reliance[1]. Stanley claimed for Arnold the credit of being the first to introduce modern history, modern languages and mathematics into the regular routine; but, here again, Shrewsbury forestalled Rugby. The truth is, that no public school ventured, of its own motion, to reform curriculum. Even the preparation of Latin and Greek grammars for common use throughout the schools, a project of Arnold in 1835, had to wait till 1866 for partial realisation in *The Public School Latin Primer*. The admission of mathematics, modern history and geography to full recognition as studies was a surrender to public opinion and a tardy imitation of the custom of commercial or 'English' schools, chiefly under private management, which educated the great majority of the middle classes. But not much came of the introduction of these studies into public schools, as the Clarendon commission of 1861—4 complained. Arnold was of opinion that it was 'not right' to leave boys and young men 'in ignorance of the beginnings of physical science'; nearly thirty years later, this royal commission was saying the same thing. The

[1] Fisher, G. W., *Annals of Shrewsbury School*, p. 362.

first steps in a real reform of courses of instruction among schools of this type were taken by the early Victorian foundations, chiefly proprietary, such as Cheltenham, Liverpool, Marlborough, Rossall, Brighton, Radley and Bradfield.

But Arnold's claim to greatness does not rest upon any purely professional achievement. His moral earnestness and strong religious conviction were naturally reflected in his administration of Rugby, as, also, was his intense belief in the responsibility of his position. His moral fervour, accompanied though it was by much heart-searching and an abiding distrust of the immaturity of boy-nature, worked an extraordinary change in the life of Rugby, and, through Rugby, in public schools and in English education at large. In his view, 'the forming of the moral principles and habits' alone constituted education, and, in this country, the process must be based on Christianity. On the latter ground, he desired the admission of all nonconformists, unitarians excepted, to the full membership of Oxford and Cambridge; and he regretfully resigned his seat (1838) in the senate of the newly created university of London because he failed to carry his colleagues with him in an acknowledgment of the paramount claim of religion in public education. He regarded with pity and apprehension the material condition of the working classes during the last years of his life; nor is it possible to measure the influence upon social reform which, at a much later time, he exercised through his pupils and admirers.

Falling trade, poor harvests, dear bread and the shock of a salutary but radical change in poor-law administration brought acute distress upon the working classes, more particularly during the years which immediately followed the passing of the first Reform bill. The consequent unrest was intensified by the feeling that that measure had not gone far enough along the road of reform. While some sought to remove or alleviate the trouble by further political or fiscal changes, others saw in the careful upbringing of the children the promise of permanent improvement. William Ellis, William Ballantyne Hodgson and Richard Dawes, dean of Hereford, hoped to remedy the evil plight of the poorer classes by careful moral training independent of religious teaching, and by 'the introduction of lessons on economical science into schools of primary instruction'; George Combe, the phrenologist, and William Lovett, the 'moral force Chartist,' were, at different times, associated with Ellis in this project. Ellis was the most active in the cause; between 1848 and 1862, he opened in London seven schools (usually called Birkbeck schools, from the fact that the first of them was held in the London Mechanics' institution[1]), instructed teachers in his aims and methods, wrote, lectured and aroused considerable interest in his ideas among teachers and school managers. The Prince Consort, in pursuance of the eclectic scheme of education which he laid down for his children, succeeded in making Ellis a sort of 'visiting master' at Buckingham palace for upwards of a year. The special feature of the Birkbeck schools was the attention given to instruction relating to bodily health and to 'the science of human well-being,' that is, the practical application of the principles of political economy to individual conduct. Most of these schools failed to compete with the board schools created by the Education act of 1870 ; one or two of them still survive as secondary schools assisted by the county council. It was a sound instinct which led Ellis to train his teachers himself ; his aims required for their attainment, as he often said, something of 'apostolic' fervour, which could not be expected from all teachers as a matter of course.

John Ruskin never ceased to denounce the blindness of political economists ; William Ellis, while confessing the charm of Ruskin and other men of letters who touched economic problems, thought that they one and all 'failed to convince.' Yet, these two men were in substantial agreement as to the kind of up-bringing which their fellow-countrymen needed. Moral training and enlightenment, bodily health, knowledge and skill applied to the daily calling were the great matters ; an intelligent apprehension of his physical surroundings, some instruction in science and mathematics, the thrifty employment of his wages, the attainment of leisure and ability to enjoy it worthily were the next important factors of the future workman's education. Ruskin, fully cognisant of the value for mental development of bodily activity and manual skill, thought 'riding, rowing and cricketing' the most useful things learned at a public school ; he would have boys of all ranks taught a handicraft. But the man of letters and the student of economics viewed the whole subject from opposite standpoints ; Ellis was thinking of the individual, Ruskin of the community. Throughout the seventeen years, dating from the appearance of *The Stones of Venice* in 1853, during which Ruskin kept the subject before the public, education and government were inseparable ideas in his mind. 'Educate or govern, they are one and the same word,' he said at Woolwich in 1869[2]. It was government's duty to provide free, universal instruction and to compel all to receive education ;

---

[1] See, *ante*, p. 28.   [2] *The Crown of Wild Olive*, par. 144.

in return, all must yield obedience to government. 'All prosperity begins in obedience[1]'; as Carlyle had said long before in *Sartor Resartus*, 'obedience is our universal duty and destiny; wherein whoso will not bend must break.' Ruskin's first object was an organised and, above all, a disciplined people; his model was the Prussian polity as shaped, first, by Frederick the great and, secondly, by Frederick William's ministers after the disaster of Jena.

The policy of reform initiated by the Oxford Examination statute of 1800 developed slowly at Oxford and Cambridge during the succeeding fifty years. At the former, the single 'school,' or examination for the degree, was made two by the institution of the mathematical school in 1807. In similar fashion, the solitary Cambridge 'tripos' (virtually a mathematical examination) became two in 1824 by the establishment of the classical tripos. At Oxford, the 'honours' and 'pass' examinations were separated, and an increasing quantity of written work was demanded from candidates. In 1850, Oxford recast its arrangements. A new test, 'The First Public Examination before Moderators' (who were empowered to award honours), was set up mid-way in the degree course, and two new schools, Natural Science and Law and Modern History were made; subsequently, the latter school became two and Theology was added. A similar recognition of modern studies was made at Cambridge in 1848 by the creation of the Moral Sciences and Natural Sciences triposes, these two examinations both comprehending a very wide range of studies. But the agitation for reform first powerfully expressed by *The Edinburgh Review* was not relaxed. Even improvements intensified it. The interest aroused by classical and mathematical examinations absorbed attention from other studies; professorial lectures were neglected in favour of teaching by college tutors, which bore directly upon the struggle for honours and degrees. At Oxford, in 1850, out of 1500 or 1600 students, the average attendance at the modern history course was eight; at the chemistry course, five and a half; at botany, six; at Arabic, none; 'medicine, Anglo-Saxon and Sanscrit are in a similar condition.' The regius professor of Greek did not lecture, no pupils offering themselves. 'Indeed the main body of professors are virtually superseded by the present system. Oxford, instead of being one great university, consists of twenty-four small universities called colleges[2].'

---

[1] *The Crown of Wild Olive*, par. 134.
[2] *A Letter to...Lord John Russell...with suggestions for a Royal Commission of*

Reformers traced most of the abuses prevalent in the universities to this subordinate position of the university corporations themselves. The heads of the college societies formed an oligarchy which, entrenched behind obsolete statutes and traditional glosses centuries old, in effect governed the university upon a basis of privilege. In closest association with the church, the authorities at Oxford excluded nonconformists absolutely, whilst Cambridge refused to admit them to degrees, the effect being to shut them out from any share in honours or powers of government. Competition for fellowships and other college emoluments was frequently nullified by statutes of endowment which restricted candidates to particular localities, schools or families. As the universities themselves were legally incompetent to change the condition of affairs, a memorial, supported by many Oxford and Cambridge graduates, was addressed, in 1850, to the prime minister, lord John Russell, requesting the appointment of a royal commission to make enquiry and suggest reform. The request was promptly granted and the commission reported in 1852. Parliamentary legislation (1854—6) and the amendment of college statutes, which it made possible, broke the college monopoly of university government, enlarged the professoriate and endowed it with college funds considered superfluous, freed colleges from obsolete obligations, in large measure threw open fellowships and other prizes and removed disabilities which prevented nonconformists from taking degrees, though without enabling them to hold fellowships. The consequence of these radical changes was an extraordinary access of new life in all branches of the universities' activity and a closer approach to the life of the nation than had been witnessed for nearly two hundred years.

The principle of undenominational education embodied in the university of London was extended to Ireland in 1845—9 by the foundation of Queen's colleges at Belfast, Cork and Galway and their incorporation as Queen's university in the next year, notwithstanding the protests of Daniel O'Connell, the Irish Roman catholic bishops and Pius IX. The hierarchy determined to establish a catholic university in Dublin and to place John Henry Newman at its head ; the university was canonically founded in 1854, Newman being its first rector. He had acted in that

Inquiry into the Universities (1850), p. 19. This pamphlet (by Row, C. A.) is a searching statement of the grievances which led to the appointment of the royal commissions of 1850—2.

capacity previous to the formal opening, and, during 1852, he delivered those addresses on the scope and nature of higher education which were published under the title, *The Idea of a University*[1]. These discourses deliberately traversed those conceptions of knowledge and of instruction which, first rendered powerful by Brougham and the utilitarians, had become very popular doctrines in the mid-century. In opposition to the demand that universities should place research and the advancement of knowledge in the forefront of their activities, Newman asserted that the chief business of a university is to teach, and in particular to illuminate the intelligence and to inculcate habits of accurate, thorough and systematic thinking. Notwithstanding its many acknowledged benefits, the diffusion of useful knowledge tended to support false, illiberal notions of what constituted instruction, to tolerate smattering and to prepare and make current 'nutshell views for the breakfast table.' While the prevailing idea was to separate theology and religious teaching from all educational institutions, Newman asserted that, as all knowledge, fundamentally, is one, the knowledge of God cannot be divorced from other forms of knowledge without causing general injury to knowledge as a whole. The elimination of theology meant that some other branch of knowledge would usurp the vacant place to its own detriment. At a time when reformers regarded professors' lectures and examinations as the most efficient mode of university education, Newman ventured upon an outspoken justification of the practice of the ancient universities and public schools, the enforcement of college residence and tutorial supervision. The moving passage in which he reverts to his Oriel days is well known ; so, too, is the taunt directed at the Baconian philosophy, 'a method whereby bodily discomforts and temporal wants are to be most effectually removed from the greatest number.' Science and literature must both occupy a great place in university education. But the former ignores sin, and the latter knows it only too well. 'It is a contradiction in terms to attempt a sinless literature of sinful man'—a home-thrust at the sixteenth-century compromise known as *pietas litterata*. Therefore, the church must fashion and mould the university's organisation, watch over its teaching, knit its pupils together and superintend its action. The suppressed premiss in this argument (an infallible church) fails to conceal the prosaic fact that the moulding and fashioning must be committed, not to

[1] See *Camb. Hist. Eng. Lit.*, vol. XII, chap. XII.

an abstract entity, but to the hands of possibly very fallible and always concrete ecclesiastics.

Shortly before parliament, in 1833, voted £20,000 *per annum* in aid of schools for the people, John Arthur Roebuck unsuccessfully moved a resolution in the commons in favour of universal, compulsory education, the professional training of teachers in normal schools and the appointment of a minister of education, in all these proposals avowedly following the example of Prussia and of France. The state policy here outlined was only partially realised during the ensuing seventy years, throughout which period it was almost continuously discussed. The appointment in 1839 of a committee of the privy council on education to 'superintend the application of any sums voted by Parliament for the purpose of promoting public education' was an assumption of direct responsibility by the state which promised to have far-reaching consequences. But the committee suffered defeat at the very outset. The first requirement of a great system of public education was the existence of a body of competent teachers. Lord Melbourne's ministry, therefore, proposed to establish a national normal school, the details of their plan being committed to the secretary of the committee, James Phillips Kay (Sir James Kay-Shuttleworth), a close student of Swiss educational practice.

In order to maintain religious instruction as an integral part of the scheme, and to respect 'the rights of conscience,' it was proposed to give both denominational and undenominational instruction in such a manner as to safeguard conscientious objectors. But this was to raise the 'religious difficulty' in connection with a policy not too popular on other grounds ; and so loud was the clamour, that the government threw over the training college scheme as a whole and confined itself to the appointment of inspectors of schools. The National society and the British and Foreign School society had, from the beginning of their history, trained their teachers ; this 'voluntary' arrangement was continued and the number of training colleges was greatly increased by different religious bodies after the government's failure in 1839. In 1846, the committee of council, still intent on the creation of a corps of teachers, materially altered the monitorial system by permitting teachers to engage apprentices, or pupil-teachers, who, after five years' service in the receipt of government pay, became eligible by examination for admission to one of the 'voluntary' training colleges, which the state aided. The system of apprenticeship for teachers has undergone great changes since its introduction ; but denominational training colleges still take part with universities and university colleges (since 1890) and municipal training colleges (since the legislation of 1902) in the preparation of teachers for the work of elementary schools.

A greater admission of state responsibility was made in 1856 by the establishment of the Education department for the supervision of elementary education; with this department was associated that of Science and Art, a public office which had been created three years earlier. The ministries of Aberdeen and Palmerston were marked by a series of abortive bills (1853—8) designed to bring public elementary instruction under public control in conjunction with expedients to meet the religious difficulty or to ignore it. Both parties to the controversy agreed that more information on the working of the existing arrangement was required, and, in 1858, the Newcastle commission was appointed for the purpose, and to report on measures likely to extend 'sound and cheap elementary instruction to all classes of the people.' The commissioners' report (1861) complained that elementary schools, as a whole, neglected the rudiments and the less capable children. Their outstanding recommendation was that the financial aid given to any school should depend, in part, upon the attainments of its pupils as determined by the inspector's examination; effect was given to this recommendation by Robert Lowe's 'revised code' of 1862, which introduced what is known as 'payment by results.' This specious phrase won public favour for a very mischievous method of administration. In the first place, as Kay-Shuttleworth strongly urged, there was no 'payment' for those moral 'results' which were the best outcome of the schoolmaster's labours, and his devotion was diverted from these to the bare rudiments of knowledge which could be assessed and paid for. The school depended for its existence upon the capacity of the children to read, write and sum; the ability to use these tools in acquiring knowledge and, still more, the manual exercises, which hitherto had formed part of the education of children of handicraftsmen and labourers, were, in consequence, thrust aside. In the struggle for grants, the teaching, neglecting the intelligent, was adapted to the lowest capacity and became very mechanical, as Matthew Arnold pointed out at an early stage in the system's history. Poorer schools, unable to employ teachers skilled in securing the highest 'results,' found, to their cost, that the watchword of the new order was *habentibus dabitur*, and their attempt to keep going was a weary business for all concerned. Until the system was abolished in 1890, attempts at improvement or palliation were, from time to time, made by the Education department in response to pressure from teachers and school-managers.

The decade preceding 1870 was notable by reason of its active interest in public instruction of all grades, and this activity was reflected in certain noteworthy books. Among these the most conspicuous was Herbert Spencer's *Education, Intellectual, Moral and Physical* (1861), in which the author collected magazine articles published by him between 1854 and 1859. The book completes a series constituted by Montaigne, Locke, Rousseau and Spencer himself, which marks the continued reaction during three centuries of French and English thought upon its special topic. Spencer's work is largely Rousseau's *Émile* in nineteenth-century English guise. Of the four chapters into which it is divided, the second, on intellectual education, is, perhaps, the most valuable; it is the nearest approach to a treatise on educational method which we have from the pen of an English writer of distinction, and much of its teaching has been absorbed into modern practice. The next chapter, on moral education, follows Rousseau, and, like *Émile*, does nothing to solve its problem. The so-called discipline of consequences as expounded by both writers would train the pupil to be wary in dealing with natural forces; but this is not morality. The fourth chapter, on physical education, has been generally recognised as sound, and as having had a valuable influence upon subsequent practice. The first chapter ('What knowledge is of most worth?'), which is a piece of special pleading for instruction in science, teems with fallacies, some of a very crude kind. Spencer appears to have been by nature unresponsive to art and literature; given this defect, and a good conceit of his own judgment, many of the author's *dicta* can be understood. But, after all, a more judicious handling of the theme of this chapter would have been quite ineffective in face of the scandalous neglect of science, as an instrument of general education, which then prevailed in this country. *Education* had an extraordinary vogue; within less than twenty years it was translated into thirteen foreign languages, including Chinese and Japanese; Spencer's great repute among the latter is well known.

The Newcastle commission of 1858—61 on the education of the poorer classes was followed by the Clarendon or Public Schools commission of 1861—4 and the Taunton or Endowed Schools commission of 1864—7; during the last named period, also, the Argyll commission investigated the condition of Scottish schools.

The Clarendon commissioners frankly recognised the improvements, moral and material, which had been made in the daily life of the nine schools to which their reference restricted them; they praised their adherence to humane letters, their discipline, moral and religious training, though they thought the schools were too tender to idlers. But the curriculum lacked breadth and variety; every boy should be taught mathematics, a branch of natural science and a modern foreign language. The Public Schools act of 1868 recast the governing bodies and gave them power to make new regulations for the management of their schools, including the provision of new studies; but, so far as the state was concerned, Winchester, Eton, St Paul's, Westminster, Harrow, Rugby, Shrewsbury, Merchant Taylors' and Charterhouse were left very much as they were before. The Taunton commission was appointed to discover measures 'for the improvement of secondary education.' Though the endowed school foundations numbered about three thousand, more than two thousand of them fell outside the purview of the commission, as they were giving purely elementary instruction. The commissioners reported a great lack of secondary schools and much inefficiency in the existing teachers, school buildings and governing bodies. They recommended a comprehensive scheme of national and local provision for, and control of, the whole sphere of education between the elementary and the public school; but parliament was content to appoint, under the Endowed Schools acts, 1869—74, commissioners with power to initiate, or amend, the schemes which controlled the operations of individual schools. This power was freely exercised until the functions of these commissioners were transferred, in 1874, to the Charity commission, with which body they remained down to 1900. Speaking generally, school schemes dealt with by both these bodies make the benefits of the school widely accessible, provide for the inclusion of modern studies, for exemption of certain pupils from religious instruction and (where necessary) for the abolition of the ancient jurisdiction of the bishop of the diocese.

The Newcastle and Taunton commissions are associated with the first steps taken by Matthew Arnold to awaken England to the defective state of such public education as it possessed. Appointed an inspector of schools in 1851, Arnold was despatched to the continent on special missions of observation by the first-named commission in 1859, and by the second in 1865. His reports (*The popular education of France with notices of that of Holland and Switzerland*, 1861, *Schools and Universities on the Continent*, 1868) concentrated attention upon the condition of the English middle class, 'nearly the worst educated in the world,' served by schools destitute of great traditions and too frequently inspired by narrow or vulgar ideals. Whereas, abroad, the commercial and industrial class participated in the highest culture of the nation, in England that class, notwithstanding its great political power, was isolated from that culture, and, being without a good standard of education in its own experience, was unable to form a just estimate of the country's needs in that respect. From the first, Arnold was struck by the high level of intellectual attainment promoted by the French *lycée* and the comparatively large area of its influence. But only the state could meet the expense of a sufficient number of these schools, supply their highly educated trained teachers and maintain a good standard by means of official inspection. The same wide extension of culture attained by similar means was observable in Germany, in Holland and in democratic Switzerland. Though the occasion of his first tour was the primary school, Arnold recognised that the organisation of elementary instruction on a national scale, apart from the consideration of secondary and higher education, would be futile as well as illogical. Hence, his first report admonished the English people to 'regard the necessities of a not distant future and *organise your secondary instruction*.' That admonition he continued to repeat throughout his official career; it concludes the report on German, Swiss and French elementary education which he drew up on his retirement in 1886. In the interval, expostulation, satire, sarcasm, persuasion, exhortation were all employed to urge the English community to assume corporate responsibility for public education as a whole ; the voluntary principle was incapable of meeting the absolute needs of a modern state. England could no more do without universal, compulsory instruction than could her neighbours.

Arnold died before the organisation of secondary education was taken in hand; but his teaching did not fail to tell in due course, as the Bryce commission of 1896 proved. In order to fix responsibility (the want of which he regarded as one of the sins of our administration generally), the national system should be presided over by a minister of education, who should be assisted by a consultative body of persons entitled to be heard on questions affecting his duties. The schools should form part of the municipal services, and, as municipal organisation did not yet exist in many parts of the country, it would have to be created. As intermediary between the localities and the ministry, 'provincial school boards,' eight or ten for the country, would ensure a national policy, which respected local wishes, while they would render unnecessary an elaborate scheme of inspection such as was employed for existing elementary schools. A school-leaving certificate, open to all secondary school pupils, would also serve as qualification for admission to the university. The universities, by offering facilities for post-graduate study, might compensate for the want of those foreign 'institutes' which trained members of the public services scientifically and, at the same time, raised the whole level of national appreciation of knowledge and the value of ideas. A comparison of the foregoing with the subsequent development of educational policy shows what Arnold's influence in these matters was.

On the long-established controversy about curriculum, Arnold took an equally comprehensive view. 'The rejection of the humanities... and the rejection of the study of nature are alike *ignorant.*' The aim of the pupil is to attain 'knowledge of himself and of the world.' Secondary schools, in their lower forms, should, therefore, provide a basis of instruction common to all pupils; above this, there should be a bifurcation, one branch for literary, the other for scientific, education. Following the model of the Prussian *Realgymnasium* (established in 1859 and since fallen into disfavour), Arnold included the elements of Latin among the common studies of all pupils; in another connection, he suggested that the Latin *Vulgate* should be studied by the more advanced pupils of elementary schools. But, of course, he was fully alive to the humanist training to be obtained from the study of modern literatures, especially that of the mother-tongue; on the other hand, he thought that instruction in speaking foreign languages was not school business.

John Stuart Mill's *Inaugural Address* to the university of St Andrews on being installed lord rector in February 1867, while not neglecting the controversies of the hour, raises the discussion about education to a level which controversies seldom reach. He agrees with Newman that British universities discharge, among other functions, that of advanced schools; but, he thinks this is owing to the absence of schools to which general education could be fully entrusted. Yet, the Scots universities have long since so organised their studies as to make an all-round education possible for their students; and 'the old English universities... are now the *foci* of free and manly enquiry to the higher and professional ꞌses south of the Tweed.' The assumed opposition between literature and science is an absurdity; anything deserving the name of a good education must include both. If classics were better taught, there would be sufficient time for the teaching of science and of 'everything else needed'; but the greater part of English classical schools are shams which fail to teach what they profess. He would not have modern languages, history or geography taught in secondary schools; the first should be learned abroad, and the other two by desultory reading. Here, he altogether fails to see the part which, by the systematic instruction of the school, these studies may be made to play in a child's development; all through the address there is ever present the recollection of his own arduous discipline (as described in his *Autobiography*) and forgetfulness of the limits to the ordinary boy's industry and power. In reference to another heated quarrel of the time, Mill roundly declares it beyond the power of schools and universities to educate morally or religiously, and then goes on to show that the home and 'society' can do this, omitting to note that schools and universities are societies, and that, from the standpoint of education, religion is not so much a philosophy or set of intellectual ideas to be taught as a life to be lived. The *Autobiography* supplies the source of the error. But Mill does not confine himself to the place of schools and universities; he passes in review the branches of culture which should be followed when education has, ostensibly, been completed. The 'aesthetic branch' of human culture is barely inferior to the other branches, the intellectual and moral; yet, the British middle class neglects it for 'commercial, money-getting business and religious puritanism,' the condition of things which, two years later, Matthew Arnold sharply flagellated in *Culture and Anarchy*. Mill's *Inaugural Address* and Newman's *Idea of a University*, when made mutually corrective, portray ideals of individual attainment which it is hard to imagine irrelevant at any stage of human civilisation.

The ground taken by Mill in reference to literature and science is that occupied by the nine distinguished writers who, under the editorship of Frederic William Farrar, published, in 1867, *Essays on a liberal education*. Henry Sidgwick, senior classic in 1859, writing on the theory of classical education, dismisses, as sophistical, many of the stock contentions in its favour; he is particularly severe when commenting on the assertions of 'the enthusiast, Mr Thring.' Sidgwick urges that the ancient authors are fine educational instruments just because their work is literature, and, on that ground, it is reasonable to employ, for a like purpose, the literature of modern tongues. He admits the claim of natural science to its place in modern education, favours the reform of methods of teaching Latin and Greek, and, in particular, would remove 'verses' from among compulsory studies, a contention to which the editor, Farrar, devotes his own essay. After the senior classic, the senior wrangler : James Maurice Wilson contributes a weighty and temperately written essay on behalf of science, which is the more convincing since it illustrates, with some detail, the serious work which boys may undertake, even when they give only two hours a week to it. John Wesley Hales, in an essay on the teaching of English, urged that a child's first notions of grammar should be derived from study of the vernacular, a rule very generally accepted at the present time. Sir John Seeley (then professor of Latin at University college, London), writing on liberal education in universities, confined himself to defects in the tutorial system of the colleges, to the baneful effects of examinations and of the exaggerated importance attached to 'triposes' and 'schools.' He suggested, as remedies, the alphabetical arrangement of all 'honours' lists, the institution of intercollegiate lectures and a greater readiness on the part of colleges to admit members of other societies to fellowships—matters of organisation now generally in operation.

Edward Thring, 'the enthusiast' of Sidgwick's essay, was headmaster of Uppingham school from 1853 till his death in 1887, during which period he raised a small, country grammar school to the educational level of the best public schools of the new foundation, he and his staff contributing nearly the whole of the capital sum required to effect the change in the material conditions of the school. To these conditions he attached high value, and he spared no pains to acquire buildings planned to meet the manifold requirements of a modern school, apparatus and appliances to advance or illustrate its studies, comely school-rooms and domestic surroundings which respected the boys' privacy. His best known book, *Theory and Practice of Teaching*, is not a professional treatise, but a series of disconnected chapters full of shrewd observation and practical hints expressed in a rugged yet epigrammatic style, which makes good reading. In his books, as in his daily work, he insisted that schools must be judged by their success in educating the dull and the mediocre boy, and not by examinations or by readiness to comply with the official craving for uniformity. Himself of a masterful disposition, he could not tolerate any interference with, or attempt to ignore, the individuality either of scholar or of school.

The Reform bill of 1832 had led the state to assume a very small measure of responsibility for public instruction; but mere trifling could not satisfy the demand for popular education heightened by the much greater extension of the parliamentary franchise effected in the bill of 1867. Nearly as many children were believed to be without schools of any kind as were in attendance at all schools, state-aided or uninspected, put together. Abortive bills and resolutions in parliament urged the imposition of an education rate, the provision of free education and the safeguard of a conscience clause in schools. Outside parliament, there was loud and persistent agitation, which centred chiefly about the question of religious instruction and the rights of conscience. Finally, in 1870, the government introduced a bill to provide for public elementary education in England and Wales, which was passed after six months of contentious debate. Its introducer, William Edward Forster, explained that its purpose was supplementary, to ensure an efficient school in every part of the kingdom, to make the erection of such schools compulsory where they did not already exist, but to use compulsion in such cases only; for this purpose, it was requisite to maintain an effectual conscience clause, undenominational inspection and a standard of efficiency in secular study. In the course of the debates, it was decided that ratepayers, not town councils or vestries, should elect school boards (the education authorities formed by the bill), to take voluntary schools out of the measure and to forbid the teaching in board schools of any formulary distinctive of a particular religious body. This last clause favoured, at the expense of all other denominations, that which was completely satisfied by bible-reading. However expedient at the moment, it was but an imperfect compromise which did not really solve the religious difficulty; it merely kept it alive. But the full significance of the Education act of 1870 lies in the fact that the English state then definitely assumed direct responsibility for public education, whose provision became a state service like that of defence or the administration of justice; it was no longer a matter of private charity conducted by the well-to-do for the benefit of the poor. For the time being, this responsibility was confined to elementary instruction; but its extension was unavoidable. The lack of schools drove most school boards into activities which rendered the 'supplementary' nature of the act a wrong description, and the boards themselves became great corporations which overshadowed the voluntary system they had been created to supplement. The principle of universally compulsory education was asserted, but it was so fenced by the permissive powers granted to the boards and by the want of schools as not unfrequently to be inoperative. The principle was enforced by an act passed in 1880, rather more than a year in advance of the French compulsory law.

Alexander Bain's *Education as a science* (1879) contains little which justifies its title. Much more is made of 'the three great functions of the intellect in the ultimate analysis—Discrimination, Agreement, Retentiveness,' than of the subject proper; while education, as an art, bulks as considerably as anything else in the book. These two parts lack cohesion. The purely psychological discussion meanders interminably, twin rocks called pleasure and pain, otherwise reward and punishment, standing up in mid-stream and everywhere visible, recalling the parental Calvinism, with its ever-present alternatives, heaven and hell. Perhaps the same grim creed accounts for Bain's opinion that 'the quint-essence of play' is 'the zest of the malevolent feeling'; Montaigne and Locke knew better. The chapters on the sequence of studies and of the intellectual powers are more to the point, yet, still, there is an exasperating diffuseness, and much which appears to be merely an *apologia* for 'hearing lessons' and for the established usage generally. The 'education values' of different studies are stated as they train intelligence or impart useful information; but they are not equated, and the results do not affect the consideration of a 'renovated curriculum' in science, the humanities and the mother-tongue. Bain was singularly un-fortunate in forecasting the trend of practice. He regarded manual instruction and bodily regimen generally as outside the school's province, thought laboratories unnecessary and hesitated about admitting history; but he devotes much attention to the now universally discredited 'object-lesson.'

The duties of Bain's chair of logic at Aberdeen included the teaching of English, work which brought him into the line of the Scottish school already mentioned[1]. Archbishop Whately's treatise, *Rhetoric* (1828), a contribution to the *Encyclopaedia Metropolitana,* had presented its subject as a branch of logic, namely argumentative composition. Bain used the term rhetoric to cover all kinds of literary composition, and, like other members of the school, tried to form a psychological groundwork for its

---

[1] See, *ante,* p. 18.

principles. While he was more successful in this respect than his predecessors, the connection between his prescriptions and the underlying laws of mental process is not always evident ; but, in the absence of a well-founded psychology of aesthetic, this is not surprising. The sharp line between composition and litera-ture drawn in Bain's latest work on rhetoric (*On teaching English,* 1887) reduces the teacher to a narrow specialist and deprives the study of letters of its highest educational office.

The great advance in the education of girls and women, which has been a prominent feature of recent educational history, may be traced back to the early activities of the Governesses' Bene-volent institution, founded in 1843. From the first, this advance has been closely connected with movements directed primarily to make teaching a profession for women. The institution soon found that it could be most helpful to governesses by making them capable of the work they undertook. For this purpose, it secured the gratuitous cooperation of F. D. Maurice and other professors of King's college, London, who began by examining women as to their fitness to teach and then, as the result of experience, conducted classes in which women could receive the necessary instruction. Queen's college, London, was founded in 1848 as a home for these classes and others for the education of girls and women ; among the first teacher-pupils were Frances Mary Buss and Dorothea Beale, who afterwards became the leaders of reform in girls' education. The relationship between King's college and Queen's college was repeated between University college and Bedford college for Women by the foundation of the latter in 1849, with a distinguished body of professors from the former as teachers, and Harriet Martineau as secretary. A committee of ladies, of which Emily Davies was secretary, induced the Taunton or Endowed Schools commission of 1864—7 to enquire into the condition of girls' schools ; the commission's report stated that, in the education of girls, there were a want of thoroughness and of system, slovenliness and showy superficiality, inattention to rudi-ments and waste of time on accomplishments which were badly taught. The remedy, obviously, was to educate the teachers and to make possible a higher education for women, for which purpose the energetic women who had the cause at heart turned to the universities. In 1865, girls were allowed to present themselves at the 'Local' examinations of Cambridge, and, in this way, periodical authoritative statements as to girls' education were made pos-sible. In 1869, Cambridge and London universities instituted examinations for women. Emily Davies then started the college at Hitchin which, in 1873, was removed to Girton; in 1869, courses of lectures were begun in Cambridge, which led to the foundation of Newnham college. A period of great expansion followed. With the help of the Endowed Schools commissioners, many girls' schools were opened or revived, many endowments on revision were divided between boys' schools and girls' schools. In 1871, 'The National Union for improving the education of women of all classes' (among whose founders lady Stanley of Alderley and Emily Shirreff, Mistress of Girton College, were prominent) took up the concurrent policy of starting good, cheap day-schools for girls and of making teaching by women a profession. The policy was realised in the creation of The Girls' Public Day School company in 1872 and of The Maria Grey Training college in 1878. The university of London threw open its degree examinations to women in 1878, Cambridge opened the triposes to them in 1881, and, three years later, Oxford allowed women to pass the examinations of certain of its 'schools.' Colleges for women had been instituted at Oxford in 1879. The new universities made no distinction of sex in respect of teaching, emoluments or degrees. The project of a women's university which animates Tennyson's *Princess* (1847) has failed to secure favour; but the less unsubstantial elements of the poet's 'medley' have come near to realisation.

No doubt, girls' schools, at the beginning, voluntarily handi-capped themselves by trying to teach most of the things taught in boys' schools, as well as those things which women either need to know, or are conventionally expected to know, or to be skilled in. But this mistake was not slow to disclose itself and be corrected. On the other hand, they were not handicapped by traditional methods; and the professional bent encouraged by the advocates of a better education for girls gave the teachers a critical attitude towards educational principles and their own work which has resulted in a high level of teaching and of organisation, and a freedom from routine. If this professional bias also tended to present teaching as the most appropriate occupation of women —which could scarcely fail to affect courses of study—later experience has reduced these early tendencies to their due proportion.

Apart from its administrative character, the relation of the colleges of Oxford and Cambridge to the universities underwent no great immediate change in consequence of the legislation of 1854—6. The energy of college tutors was expended on the education of undergraduates; it was almost a commonplace of speakers and writers that, in striking contrast with some foreign universities, Oxford and Cambridge produced but little original work in science or learning. No reformers were more dissatisfied with the state of affairs than many of the university teachers themselves. Newman believed that a university could not at the same time be a place of education and a home of research and learning; Mark Pattison, on the contrary, boldly asserted that, unless teachers were actively engaged in advancing knowledge, their teaching would be inadequate and barren.

All attempts to stimulate the teaching activity [of Oxford] without adding to its solid possession of the field of science will only feed the unwholesome system of examinations which is now undermining the educational value of the work we actually do[1].

As Pattison read the early history of colleges, their founders intended them for the promotion of learning and the technical instruction of priests, ecclesiastical lawyers and men of affairs; the most urgently needed reform was the appropriation of a large part of the college revenues to the encouragement of research and the provision of the highest type of scientific technical instruction. It was Pattison's hope that such a readjustment of finances would ensure a numerous body of fairly paid teachers, who would have time and opportunity to continue their own studies, to the advantage of the world beyond their own lecture rooms. The act of 1877, which appointed, in both universities, commissions with executive powers to deal with college statutes, rendered possible the partial realisation of this policy. The abolition of religious tests at Oxford, Cambridge and Durham in 1871 removed the last disability which rested upon nonconformists, with the double advantage of admitting them into the full current of national education and of rendering university life a truer mirror of the life of the nation at large. The greatly increased activities of both universities since 1870 are reflected in the number and variety of 'schools' and 'triposes' instituted since that date.

The growth of 'university colleges' (under this or some similar name), which was remarkable during the period 1872—84, was the result of the development of physical science, of a better appreciation of the dependence of industry upon science and a more widely extended faith in the power conferred by knowledge and intellectual cultivation, added to a growing sense of our national deficiencies in these respects. In some places, these

[1] *Suggestions on academical organisation* (1868).

currents of opinion were strengthened or liberalised by 'university extension,' the movement in favour of which was due, in the first place, to the desire, already described, of making teaching a profession for women. In 1867, James Stuart was invited to give lectures to women on the art of teaching. He preferred, however, to deliver a course on astronomy, which he repeated in several of the great northern cities. These lectures proved the existence of a demand for teaching which Cambridge met in the following year by inaugurating the plan of extra-mural lecturing and tuition, a plan adopted by the London society (instituted in 1876) and by Oxford in 1878. The development of all these new centres of intellectual life led, in due course, to the creation of new universities, none of which is confined to the study of science, applied or pure, while some have already made notable contributions to the advancement of letters in many directions.

Owens college, founded so far back as 1851 in response to demands very like those which had led to the creation of the university of London, was the earliest of the university colleges outside the capital to seek academical independence. In 1880, a royal charter was granted to Victoria university with its seat in Manchester, and Owens college was, at first, its only college. In 1884, it was joined by University college, Liverpool, and, in 1887, by the Yorkshire college, Leeds, as constituted colleges of the university. A university charter having been granted to Mason's college, Birmingham, in 1900, the three colleges of Victoria university were by fresh charters created the Victoria university of Manchester (1903), the university of Liverpool (1903) and that of Leeds (1904) respectively. The university of Sheffield was founded in 1905, and that of Bristol in 1909. University college, Dundee, had been affiliated to the university of St Andrews in 1897 ; and the Irish university system had been remodelled in 1880 and 1908—9.

The University of London act of 1898 led to the restoration of its teaching function and the possibility of unifying the higher education of the metropolis. It is worth remarking that, of the eleven universities now existing south of Tweed, nine were founded later than the reign of George IV. ' I wish we had several more universities,' said Seeley, ' our material progress has outrun our intellectual[1].' The worship of material success and the indifference to ' ideas ' with which Mill, Arnold, Pattison, Seeley and others charged the English middle class are, perhaps, not much less

---

[1] *Essays on a liberal education* (1867).

prevalent today than they were fifty years ago; but the agents for overcoming them and the reasons why they should be overcome have, in the interval, been greatly multiplied.

Wales preceded England in the organisation of secondary education. The Welsh Intermediate Education act of 1889 gave the principality a scheme which filled the gap between public elementary schools and her three colleges, Aberystwyth, Cardiff and Bangor; the system was completed by the incorporation of these colleges as the university of Wales in 1893. English legislation of 1889—90, dealing with technical instruction, brought about a chaos which rendered organisation imperative. The immediate consequence of the acts of parliament was to stimulate the Science and Art department's mischievous system of examination grants, the transformation of all but the strongest grammar schools into schools of science, the entire discouragement of literary instruction and ruinous competition between new and old institutions. The great school boards, assisted by the Education department, had endeavoured to compensate for the lack of secondary education within their areas by the creation of 'higher grade schools,' which, in some respects, partook of the nature of secondary schools, while, in others, they resembled the higher primary schools of the continent. These, also, became competitors, in some places, with the older schools under boards of governors, while they bred confusion in the public mind as to the respective functions of 'elementary' and 'secondary' instruction. The Bryce commission, appointed in 1894 to review the whole field of secondary instruction, reported in 1895, the chief measures proposed being first, the creation of a Board of Education, under a minister, to absorb the functions of the Education department, the Science and Art department and the educational side of the Charity commission, the new body thus becoming the central authority for elementary, technical and secondary education; second, the institution of a consultative committee of independent persons competent to advise the minister; and the erection in counties and county boroughs of Local Education authorities. In the meantime, 'voluntary schools' had fallen into financial distress and denominational education suffered correspondingly. The general policy long before indicated by Matthew Arnold, reiterated by the Bryce commission and emphasised by the condition of the country and the menace of foreign competition was at length embodied in the Board of Education act of 1899 and the Education acts of 1902—3. The English state had, after a century of hesitation, consented to accept full responsibility for national education.

BIBLIOGRAPHY

EDUCATION

See, also, Camb. Hist. Eng. Lit., vol. IX, pp. 568–574.

I. HISTORY OF EDUCATION: HISTORIES AND ILLUSTRATIVE WRITINGS

(a) General

Adams, Sir John. The Evolution of Educational Theory. 1912.

Adams, Francis. History of the Elementary School Contest in England. 1882.

Adamson, J. W. A short history of education. Cambridge, 1919.

Almond, Hely Hutchinson. Mr Lowe's Educational Theories examined from a practical point of view. Edinburgh, 1868.

Balfour, Graham. The educational systems of Great Britain and Ireland. 2nd edn. 1903.

Bell, Andrew. An experiment in education made at the Male Asylum of Madras. 1797.
  An address to the public in recommendation of the Madras system (by Hollingsworth, N. J.). 1812.

Binns, Henry Bryan (ed.). A century of education, being the centenary history of the British and Foreign School Society. 1908.

Birchenough, C. History of elementary education in England and Wales from 1800. 1914.

Bowen, H. C. Froebel and education by self-activity. 1893.

Bowles, John. A letter addressed to Samuel Whitbread, Esq., M.P., in consequence of the unqualified approbation...of Mr Lancaster's system of education, etc. 1807.

Brown, John. A memoir of Robert Blincoe, an orphan boy sent...to endure the horrors of a cotton-mill. Manchester, 1832.

Bruce, H. A. (afterwards lord Aberdare). An address delivered to the National Association for the promotion of Social Science. 1866.

Close, Francis (Dean of Carlisle). National Education. The secular system, the Manchester Bill and the Government scheme considered. 1852.

Collet, C. D. History of the taxes on knowledge. 2 vols. 1899.

Connoisseur, The. No. 22 (1754). The modern method of education. (Colman, G. and Langton, B.)

Cowper, William. Tirocinium. 1784.

Craik, Sir Henry. The State in its relation to Education. New edn. 1914.

Darton, F. J. Harvey. Bell and the Dragon. Fortnightly Review. May 1909.

Davies, Geo. History and mystery of the Scarborough Lancasterian Schools.
Scarborough, 1840.
—— Sequel to the history, etc. 2 pts. 1842-3.
Davies, John Llewelyn. The Working Men's College, 1854-1904. 1904.
Denison, Geo. Anthony. The Church of England and the Committee of
Council on Education. 2nd edn. 1849.
—— Supplement to Appendix B of a reply to the...promoters of the Man-
chester and Salford education scheme. 1852.
—— Notes of my life, 1805-78. 2nd edn. Oxford, 1878. (Eton and Christ
Church.)
Emery, Thomas. Educational economy, or State education vindicated. 1849.
Fox, Wm Johnson. On the educational clauses in the Bill...for the edu-
cation of children in factory districts. 2nd edn. 1843. [Sir James
Graham's bill.]
Frend, Wm. A plan of universal education. 1832.
Garfit, A. Some points of the education question, with outline of the...
progress of popular education. 1862.
—— The Conscience Clause. 1868.
Grant, James. History of the Burgh Schools of Scotland. 1876.
Gregory, Robert. Elementary education: its rise in England. 1895.
Hill, Frederic. National education, its present state and prospects. 2 vols.
1836.
Hinton, John Howard. A review of the evidence...in relation to the state of
education in Manchester and Salford. 1852.
—— A few plain words on the two Education Bills. 1852.
Hodgson, Geraldine Emma. Rationalist English Educators. 1912.
—— A study in illumination. (Wm Wordsworth.) 1914.
Holland, Henry Wilkinson. Proposed national arrangements for primary
education. 3rd edn. 1870.
Hook, Walter Farquhar (dean of Chichester). On the means of rendering
more efficient the education of the people. 1846.
Hoppus, John. Thoughts on academical education and degrees in arts. 1837.
—— Crisis of popular education. 1847.
Lamb, Charles. The old and the new schoolmaster.
Lancaster, Joseph. Outlines of a plan for educating ten thousand poor
children. 1806.
—— An account of the progress of Joseph Lancaster's plan. 1809.
—— The British System of Education. 1810.
—— Instructions for forming...a society for the education of the labouring
classes. 1810.
—— Schools for all. 1812.
    A few notes...relative to Joseph Lancaster's plan (by Eccletus). 1806.
    A vindication of Mr Lancaster's system (by Pythias). 1812.
    Common Sense *versus* Lancaster (by Collyer, N.). 1812.
    Epitome of some of the chief events in the life of Joseph Lancaster.
      New Haven. 1833.
Leach, A. F. Art. Schools. Encycl. Brit., 11th edn. Vol. xxiv.
Liberal, Letitia. A defence of Joseph Lancaster and the Royal British
system. 1810.
Lounger, The. Edinburgh, No. 67 (1786). Modern education superior to
ancient. (Mackenzie, Henry.)
Manchester Literary and Philosophical Society. Memoirs. Vol. ii. 1783.
Improvement of liberal education in Manchester.
Mansbridge, Albert. University Tutorial Classes. 1913.
Mantoux, Paul. La révolution industrielle au xviii⁰ siècle. Paris, 1906.

Marsh, Herbert. The National Religion the Foundation of National Education. A Sermon. 1811. [Ptd in The Pamphleteer, vol. I, 1813.]
—— A vindication of Dr Bell's system of education. 1811.
Maurice, J. Frederick Denison. The Educational Magazine. 1835, etc.
—— A letter to the bishop of London in reply to the article in No. 172 of the Quarterly Review. 1850.
—— The Christian Socialist. 1851, etc.
—— Plan of a female college. Cambridge, 1855.
—— A few words on secular and denominational education. 1870.
Mirror, The. Edinburgh. No. 15 (1779). A classical contrasted with a fashionable education. (Home, J.)
—— No. 106 (1780). Education for leisure. (Craig.)
—— Nos. 88 and 97–8 (1780). The private tutor. (Craig and lord Hailes.)
Moore, H. Kingsmill. An unwritten chapter in the history of Education... 1811–31. 1904.
Morley (viscount). The struggle for national education. 1873.
Observer, The. Nos. 36–7. Public School education. (Cumberland, Richard.)
Owen, Rob. Dale. An outline of the system of education in New Lanark. 1824.
Pole, Thomas. Observations on Infant Schools. Bristol, 1823.
Prideaux, E. B. R. A survey of elementary English education. 1915.
Rowntree, J. W. and Binns, H. B. A history of the Adult School Movement. 1903.
Sadler, M. E. Continuation Schools in England and elsewhere. 1907. (With a bibliography.)
—— Syllabus of a course on the history of education in England. 1800–1911. Manchester, 1911.
Salmon, David, and Hindshaw, W. Infant Schools: their history and theory. 1904.
Sexton, A. H. The First Technical College: a sketch of the history of 'The Andersonian.' 1894.
Shaw, Wm (rector of Chelvey, Somerset). Suggestions respecting a plan of national education. Bath, 1801.
Southey, Robert. Essays, moral and political. 2 vols. 1832. Essay IX. On the means of improving the people. 1818.
Thompson, J. Forty four years of the education question, 1870–1914. 1914.
Toynbee, Arnold. Lectures on the Industrial Revolution of the eighteenth century in England. 1908.
Trimmer, Sarah. The Oeconomy of Charity. 2 vols. 1801. (Greatly enlarged from the edition of 1786.)
Walsh, Wm John, archbishop. The Irish University question. Dublin, 1890.
Welton, James. Educational Theory, s.v. Education. Encyc. Brit. 11th edn. Vol. VIII.
Wilson, William. System of infants' education. 2 vols. 2nd ed. 1825.
—— A manual of instruction for Infants' Schools. 1829.
Wodehouse, Helen. A survey of the History of Education. 1924.

(b) *Universities*

Davies, Richard. Epistle to... Dr Hales on the general state of education in the universities. Bath, 1759.
—— Observations on the present state of the English universities occasion'd by Dr Davies' account. 1759.
Ollard, S. L. The Six Students of St Edmund Hall expelled... in 1768. (With a bibliography.) 1911.

A collection of papers designed to ... vindicate ... the subscription required by the University of Oxford. Oxford, 1772.

Reflections on the impropriety ... of lay subscription. Oxford [1772].

[Randolph, T.] 'An answer' to the fore-going. Oxford [1772].

Kippis, A. A vindication of the protestant dissenting ministers with regard to their late application to Parliament. 2nd edn. 1773.

Tucker, J. Letters to the Rev. Dr Kippis. 1773.

Knox, V. 'On some parts of the discipline in our English universities,' *in* Essays, moral and literary. 1782.

Disney, John. Works of John Jebb. Vol. I, pp. 182–222 on the subscription question. 1787.

Frend, Wm. Thoughts on subscription to religious tests. St Ives, 1788–9.

Considerations on the ... injuries arising from the course of education pursued in the Universities ... and public schools. 1832.

Turton, Thos. (bishop of Ely). Thoughts on the admission of persons, without regard to their religious opinions, to certain degrees in the universities of England. Cambridge, 1834.

Lee, Samuel. Some remarks on the Dean of Peterborough's tract, 'Thoughts, etc.' Cambridge, 1834.

Thirlwall, Connop. A letter to the Revd Thos. Turton on the admission of dissenters to academical degrees. Cambridge, 1834.

—— A second letter to the Revd Thomas Turton. Cambridge, 1834.

Whewell, Wm. Remarks on some parts of Mr Thirlwall's letter. Cambridge, 1834.

—— Additional remarks on some parts of Mr Thirlwall's two letters. Cambridge, 1834.

Sedgwick, A. Admission of Dissenters to academical degrees. Cambridge Chronicle 9 June 1834.

Rose, Henry John. Letter on foregoing subject to Cambridge Chronicle 10 June 1834.

Sewell, Wm. Thoughts on the admission of dissenters to the University of Oxford. Oxford, 1834.

—— A second letter to a Dissenter on the opposition of the University of Oxford to the charter of the London College. Oxford, 1834.

—— The attack upon the University of Oxford in a letter to Earl Grey. 2nd edn. 1834.

—— Collegiate reform. A sermon. Oxford, 1838.

—— The Nation, the Church and the University of Oxford. Two sermons. Oxford, 1849.

Gray, John Hamilton. The admission of dissenters into the universities considered. Oxford, 1834.

Wordsworth, Christopher. On the admission of dissenters to reside and graduate. Cambridge, 1834.

Blakesley, Jos. Williams. The studies of the University essentially general. Cambridge, 1836.

—— Thoughts on the recommendations of the Ecclesiastical Commission. 1837.

An historical vindication of ... Earl Radnor's bill ... to inquire respecting the statutes and administration of the colleges and halls. 1837. Anon.

Whewell, Wm. On the principles of university education. 1837.

—— Liberal education, with particular reference to the University of Cambridge. 1845.

A Layman. The independence of the universities and colleges. Oxford, 1838.

Huber, Victor Aimé. The English Universities. Abridged translation by Newman, F. W. 2 vols. in 3. 1843.

Amos, Andrew. Four lectures on the advantages of a classical education as an auxiliary to a commercial education. 1846.

Manning, W. Oke. Remarks upon religious tests at the English universities. 1846.

Arnold, Thos, and others. Opinions on the admission of dissenters to the universities and on university reform. 1847.

Newman, John Henry (cardinal). *See* Camb. Hist. Eng. Lit., bibliography to chapter XII, volume XII.

[Bain, Alex.] University Education, *in* Westminster Review, July 1848. (Reviewing Whewell's Liberal Education.)

Seeley, Sir John. Liberal Education in Universities. *See* Essays on a Liberal Education. 1867.

Pattison, Mark, and others. Essays on the endowment of research. 1876.

Campbell, Lewis. The nationalisation of the old English universities. 1901.

Mullinger, Jas Bass. Art. Universities, Encycl. Brit. 11th edn. Vol. XXVII.

Raleigh, Sir Walter Alexander. Meaning of a university. 1911.

Tillyard, A. I. A history of university reform from 1800. Cambridge, 1913.

The study of English and other modern literatures:

 Quarterly Review, vols. CLXIII–CLXIV, 1886-7.

 Nettleship, Henry. Study of modern European languages and literatures in... Oxford. 1887.

 Collins, J. Churton. The study of English literature. 1891.

 Firth, C. H. The School of English language and literature. Oxford, 1909.

Aberdeen

Fasti Aberdonenses: selections from the records of the University and King's College of Aberdeen, 1494-1854. Spalding Club, No. 26. 1854.

Rectorial addresses delivered in the Universities of Aberdeen, 1835-1900. Ed. Anderson, P. J. Aberdeen, 1902.

Grant Duff, Sir M. E. Inaugural addresses delivered to the University of Aberdeen. Edinburgh, 1867.

Maclean, Neil N. Life at a northern university. Ed. Leask, W. K. Aberdeen, 1906.

Cambridge

A sincere well wisher. Free thoughts upon university education. 1751.

Connoisseur, The. No. 41 (1754). Newmarket as a supplement to the University of Cambridge (Colman, G. & Thornton, B.).

—— No. 107 (1756). Excessive mathematics at Cambridge.

Idler, The. No. 33 (1758). Journal of a Fellow of a College (Warton, T.).

—— No. 67 (1759). Scholar's Journal (Langton, B.).

Ingram, Robert Acklom. The necessity of introducing divinity into the regular course. Colchester, 1792.

Gentleman's Magazine, The. Apr., May 1774, Dec. 1792, Jan., Feb., July 1793. On studies at Cambridge.

Anon. Strictures upon the discipline of the University of Cambridge. Cambridge, 1792.

Pembrochian. Gradus ad Cantabrigiam, or a dictionary of terms used at the University of Cambridge. 1803.

Wainewright, Latham. The literary and scientific pursued... encouraged and enforced in the University of Cambridge. 1815.

Eubulus [Samuel Butler of Shrewsbury]. Thoughts on the present system of academic education. 1822.

—— A letter to Philograntus. 1822.

Philograntus [Jas Hen. Monk]. A letter...on the additional examination of students. 1822.

A Brace of Cantabs. Gradus ad Cantabrigiam, or new university guide to the academical customs and colloquial or cant terms. 1824.

[Wright, J. M. F.] Alma mater, or seven years at the University of Cambridge by a Trinity-man. 1827.

Sedgwick, Adam. A discourse on the studies of the University. 1833.

Selwyn, Wm. Extracts from college examinations in divinity...with a letter to the lecturers and examiners. Cambridge, 1834.

Resident member of the University. Hints for the introduction of an improved course of study in the University. Cambridge, 1835.

Walsh, Benj. Dann. A historical account of the university of Cambridge and its colleges: in a letter to the earl of Radnor. 1837.

Peacock, Geo. Observations on the statutes of the University. 1841.

Members of the University. Cambridge Essays. 1855-8.

[Stephen, Sir Leslie.] Sketches from Cambridge, by a Don. 1865.

Roberts, Robert Davies. Eighteen years of university extension. 1891.

Dublin

The Book of Trinity College, Dublin. Belfast, 1892.

Vickers, Robert. Praelection...on the university system of education. Dublin, 1849.

Edinburgh

Grant, Sir Alex. The story of the University of Edinburgh during its first three hundred years. 2 vols. 1884.

Stodart-Walker, A. (editor). Rectorial addresses delivered before the University, 1859-99. 1900.

Edinburgh Essays. 1858.

Glasgow

Coutts, Jas. A history of the University of Glasgow from its foundation in 1451. Glasgow, 1909.

Hay, John Barras (ed.). Inaugural addresses by Lords Rectors of the University. 1839.

Ireland

Nemo. A few words on the new Irish Colleges. 1845.

Andrews, Thos. Address on Education to the Social Science Association. 1867.

—— Studium Generale, a chapter of contemporary history. 1867. (University of London, the new Irish universities, Maynooth.)

London

Beattie, Wm. Life and letters of Thos. Campbell. 3 vols. 1849. (Vol. II, chap. xiv.)

Christianus. Letter to...Robert Peel...on the University of London, 1828. See, also, Quarterly Review, vol. XXXIX, 1829.

Quarterly Review, vol. CLXIV, 1887.

Oxford

Bentham, Ed. Letter to a young gentleman of Oxford. 1748.

—— Letter to a fellow of a college. 1749.

Evans, Margaret (ed.). Letters of Richard Radcliffe and John James of Queen's College, Oxford. 1753-83. Oxf. Hist. Soc., 1888.

[Warton, Thos.] A companion to the guide and a guide to the companion. [1762?]

[Napleton, John.] Considerations on the residence usually required for degrees in the University. Oxford, 1772.

—— Considerations on the public exercises for the first and second degrees. Oxford, 1773.

Philalethes. A letter to the Rev. V. Knox on...his animadversions on the University. Oxford, 1790.

[Copleston, Edward.] A reply to the calumnies of the Edinburgh Review. Oxford, 1810.

—— A Second Reply. Oxford, 1810.

—— A Third Reply. Oxford, 1811.

Hamilton, Sir Wm. Discussions on philosophy and literature, education and university reform. Chiefly from the Edinburgh Review. 3rd edn. 1866.

A Member of Convocation [Vaughan Thomas]. The legality of the present academical system...asserted against the new calumnies of the Edinburgh Review. Oxford, 1831.

—— The legality etc....reasserted. Oxford, 1832.

Tuckwell, Wm. Pre-Tractarian Oxford: a reminiscence of the Oriel 'Noetics.' 1909.

—— Reminiscences of Oxford. 1900.

Davison, John. Remains and occasional publications. Oxford, 1840.

John Duke, baron Coleridge. Memorials of Oxford (verse). Oxford, 1844.

Maurice, J. F. D. The new statute and Mr Ward. Oxford, 1845.

Country Schoolmaster. A Letter to the authors of 'Suggestions for an improvement of the Examination Statute.' Oxford, 1848.

Walker, Robert. A letter...on improvements in the present examination statute and the studies of the University. Oxford, 1848.

A Member of the Oxford Convocation [C. A. Row]. Letter to...Lord John Russell...on the constitutional defects of the University and colleges of Oxford, with suggestions for a Royal Commission. 1850.

Row, Chas. Adolphus. Letter to Sir Robert H. Inglis...in reply to his speech on University reform. 1850.

[Sewell, Wm.] The University Commission, or Lord John Russell's post-bag. Oxford, 1850.

Price, Bonamy. Suggestions for the extension of professorial teaching. 1850.

Wilson, Henry Bristow. A letter to the...Chancellor of the University... on University and college reform. 1854.

Barry, Hen. Boothby. Remarks on the three proposals for reforming the constitution of the University. Oxford, 1854.

Barrow, John. The case of Queen's College, Oxford. Oxford, 1854.

Members of the University. Oxford Essays. 1855.

Acland, Sir Thos. Dyke. Some account of the origin and objects of the new Oxford examinations for the title of Associate in Arts. 1858.

Cox, Geo. Val. Recollections of Oxford. 1858.

Moore, Edward. Frugal education attainable under the existing collegiate system. Oxford, 1867.

Smith, Goldwin. Plea for the abolition of tests in the University. Oxford, 1864.

—— Re-organisation of the University. Oxford, 1868.

—— Oxford and her colleges. 1894.

Pattison, Mark. Suggestions on academical organization. 1868.

Mozley, Thomas. Reminiscences, chiefly of Oriel College and the Oxford movement. 2 vols. 1882.

Mackinder, H. J. and Sadler, M. E. University extension, past, present and future. 3rd ed. 1891.

Curzon of Kedleston, lord. Principles and methods of university reform. Oxford, 1909.

Victoria University, Manchester

Owens College, Essays and Addresses by Professors of. 1874.⌐

Thompson, Joseph. The Owens College, its foundation and growth and its connection with the Victoria University, Manchester. Manchester, 1886.

Hartog, P. J. Owens College, Manchester: a brief history of the College. 1900.

Roscoe, Sir H. E. The life and experiences of, written by himself. 1906.

St Andrews

Knight, Wm (ed.). Rectorial addresses at St Andrews University, 1863–1893. 1894.

Votiva Tabella: memorial volume of St Andrews University, 1411–1911. 1911.

Donaldson, Sir James. Addresses delivered in the University of St Andrews from 1886 to 1910. Edinburgh, 1911.

(c) Schools

A Carthusian [Smythe, Robert]. Historical account of the Charterhouse. 1808.

A Carthusian [Roper, W. J. D.]. Chronicles of Charterhouse. 1847.

Haig Brown, Wm. Charterhouse, past and present. Godalming, 1879.

Clifton College Register, 1862–1887, compiled by Oakeley, E. M.: historical preface by Wilson, J. M. 1887.

Clifton College Annals and Register, 1862–1912. Edited by Borwick, F. Introduction by King, J. E. Bristol, 1912.

Christ's Hospital, Annals of, by Pearce, E. H. 1901.

Lamb, Charles. Christ's Hospital Five and Thirty Years Ago.
    Recollections of Christ's Hospital [1782–9].

Edinburgh, History of the High School of, by Steven, Wm. 1849.

Austen Leigh, R. A. Eton under Barnard, 1754–65. Eton, 1904.

—— A list of Eton College in 1771 (including time-tables). Eton, 1903.

Gregory Griffin [Canning, Geo. and others]. The Microcosm, a periodical work. 40 nos. 1786–7.

Doyle, Sir Francis Hastings. Reminiscences and Opinions, 1813–85. 1886.

Wilkinson, Chas. Allix. Reminiscences of Eton (Keate's time). 1888.

Selwyn, Thos. Kynaston. Eton in 1829–30. Edited with translation [from the Greek] and notes by Warre, Edmond.

The Eton system of education vindicated. 1834.

Eton Addresses [verse]. Eton, 1831–6, 1840.

The Eton Observer, a miscellany conducted by present Etonians. Eton, 1860.

Johnson, Wm (Cory, Wm). Hints for Eton masters, 1862. London, 1898.

Collins, W. L. Etoniana, ancient and modern. 1865.

O. E. Eton under Hornby [1868–84]. 1910.

[Bankes, G. N.] A day of my life ... by an Eton boy. 1877.

Parker, Eric. Eton in the Eighties. 1914.

Ainger, A. C. Eton in prose and verse. (Historical introduction.) 1910.

Thornton, Percy Melville. Harrow School and its surroundings. 1885.

Bowen, Edward Ernest (1836–1901). Harrow Songs and other verses. 1886.
    See, also, post, 1 (e).

Howson, Edmond W. and Warner, G. T. Harrow School. 1898.

Butler, Josephine E. Recollections of George Butler. Bristol, 1892. (Harrow and Cheltenham.)
    See, also, under Winchester.

Christ Church, Manchester. The Charters of the Collegiate Church, the Free Grammar School, etc. 1791.
Manchester Free Grammar School: by an old scholar. 1849.

Marlborough College, a History of, by Bradley, A. G., Champneys, A. C., Baines, J. W. 1893.
Lockwood, Edw. Early days of Marlborough College. 1893.

Merchant Taylors' School, History of, by Wilson, H. B. 2 vols. 1812-4.

Sewell, Wm. A Year's Sermons ... preached in ... St Peter's College, Radley. 2 vols. Oxford, 1854-69.
Close, Francis. High Church education delusive and dangerous, being an exposition of the system adopted by W. Sewell. 1855.

Rossall School, History of, by Rowbotham, John Fdk. Manchester, 1894.

Rouse, W. H. D. A History of Rugby School. 1898.
Nimrod [Chas Jas Apperley]. Life and Times. *See* Fraser's Magazine. Vol. XXVI. 1842. (Rugby under James.)
Landor, Walter Savage: a biography by John Forster. 2 vols. 1869. (Rugby under James.)
Cotton, Sophia Anne. Memoir of Geo. Edwd Lynch Cotton. 1871. (Rugby under Arnold: also Westminster 1825-32, and Marlborough.)
Wratislaw, A. H. A plea for the ancient charitable foundation of Rugby School. 1864.

Sedbergh. History of the parish and grammar school, by Platt, E. A. Kendal, 1876.

Shrewsbury School. Annals of, by Fisher, G. W.
Butler, Samuel. A letter to Henry Brougham, Esq. 1820.

Tonbridge School. The History of, by Rivington, Septimus. 3rd edn. 1910.

Forshall, F. H. Westminster School, past and present. 1884.
Vincent, W. A defence of public education. 1802.
Layman, A. Remarks on Vincent's Defence. 1802.
Morrice, D. An attempted reply to the Master of Westminster School. 1802.
Albemarle, 6th earl of. Fifty years of my life. 2 vols. 1876.
Williamson, Richard. A short account of the discipline, studies, examinations, prizes etc. of Westminster School. 1845.

Kirby, Thomas Fdk. Annals of Winchester College from 1382. 1892.
Edgeworth, Maria. The Barring Out. 1806. (Winchester 'rebellion,' of 1793.)
Wordsworth, Charles. Annals of my early life, 1806-46. 1891. (Harrow, Oxford, Winchester.)
Bowles, W. L. Vindiciae Wykehamicae ... in a letter to Henry Brougham. 2nd ed. 1819. (The Pamphleteer. Vol. XIII.)
Malet, Sir Alexander. Some account of fagging at Winchester. 1828.
    An old Etonian. Letter to Sir Alexander Malet. 1829.
    Quarterly Review, vol. XXXIX. 1829.
Trollope, Thomas Adolphus. What I remember. 3 vols. 1877-9. (Harrow, Winchester, 1820-8.)

How, Fred. Douglas. Six great schoolmasters. (Eton, Winchester, Shrewsbury, Harrow, Rugby, Marlborough.) [1904.]

Mozley, Thos. Reminiscences, chiefly of towns, villages and schools. 2 vols. 1885.

Nonconformist Academies

Harrison, Ralph. A sermon preached at Manchester on the ... establishment of an academy. Together with a discourse ... at the public commencement of the academy by T. Barnes. Warrington [1786].

Rees, A. The advantages of knowledge ... recommended ... to the supporters of a new academical institution among protestant dissenters. 1788.

Harrison, Ralph. Sermons on various important subjects: with life of the author by W. Harrison. Manchester, 1813.

Turton, Thos. A review of the principal dissenting colleges in England during the last century. 1835. (Alternative title: 'Thoughts on the admission of persons ... to certain degrees,' etc.) See *ante*, p. 57.

(d) *Education of Girls and Women*

Ballard, Geo. Memoirs of several ladies of Great Britain ... celebrated for their writings or skill in the learned languages, arts and sciences. Oxford, 1752.

Beale, Dorothea. On the education of girls. Paper at the Social Science Congress. 1866. Reports issued by the Schools Inquiry Commission on the education of girls. 1869.

—— On the organisation of girls' day schools. Paper at the Social Science Congress. 1873.

—— Work and play in girls' schools. 1898. (With Soulsby, L. H. M., and Dove, J. F.)

—— Addresses to Teachers. 1908.

　　Dorothea Beale of Cheltenham (1831-1905): by Raikes, Elizabeth. 1908.

Booth, James. On the female education of the industrious classes. 1855.

Bremner, Christina S. Education of girls and women in Great Britain. 1897.

Broadhurst, Frances. A word in favor of female schools. (The Pamphleteer. Vol. XXVII.) 1826.

Broadhurst, Thos. Advice to young ladies on the improvement of the mind. 1808.

Burstall, Sara A. and Douglas, M. A. (edd.). Public Schools for girls. 1911.

Buss, Frances Mary. F. M. B. and her work for education, by Ridley, Annie E. 1895.

—— Frances Mary Buss Schools' Jubilee Record: Eleanor M. Hill and Sophie Bryant. 1900.

　　See Gurney, Mary.

Cartwright, Mrs. Letters on female education addressed to a married lady. 1777.

Chapone, Mrs (Mulso, Hester). Letters on the improvement of the mind. 2 vols. 1777.

Clough, Blanche Athena. A memoir of Anne Jemima Clough. 1897.

Cobbe, Frances Power. Life as told by herself. 1904.

—— Female education. Paper at Social Science Congress. 1862.

Davies, Emily. The application of funds to the education of girls. [1865.]

—— Women in the universities of England and Scotland. 1896.

—— Thoughts on some questions relating to women, 1860-1908. 1910.

[Edgeworth, Maria.] Letters for literary ladies. 1795.

[Fielding, Sarah.] The Governess, or the little female academy. [n.d. 1765 or earlier.]

Gregory, John. A father's legacy to his daughters. 1774. (Many edd. till 1877.)

Grey, Mrs William. [Maria Georgina Grey, born Shirreff.] The Education of Women. 1871.

—— The study of education as a Science. Paper at British Association. 1874.

Grey, Mrs William and Shirreff, Emily A. E. Thoughts on self-culture addressed to women. 2 vols. 1850.

Gurney, Mary. Are we to have education for middle-class girls? The history of Camden Collegiate Schools. 1872.

Hamilton, Elizabeth (author of The Cottagers of Glenburnie). Letters on the elementary principles of education. 2 vols. Bath, 1801. 6th ed. 1818.

—— Hints addressed to patrons and directors of schools. 1815. (Pestalozzi's principles.)

Hodgson, Wm Ballantyne. The education of girls considered in connexion with university local examinations. A lecture. 1864.

Knox, V. Liberal Education. 1781. Section XXVII.

Lounger, The. Edinburgh, 1785-6. Nos. 13 (McLeod Bannatyne), 16 (Tytler, Wm), 52 (William Craig).

Macaulay, Mrs Catherine, born Sawbridge. Letters on education. 1790.

Maurice, J. Frederick Denison. Queen's College, London, its object and method. 1848.

Quarterly Review, vols. LXXXIV, LXXXVI. 1848-50.

Maynard, Constance L. From early Victorian schoolroom to university. Nineteenth Century and After. Nov. 1914.

Mirror, The. Edinburgh, 1780. Nos. 89 and 96 (latter by Mackenzie, Henry).

More, Hannah. Strictures on Female Education, 1799. See vols. V and VI of Works, new edn. 11 vols. 1830.

—— Memoirs of the life and correspondence of H. M.: by Roberts, Wm. 3rd ed. 4 vols. 1835.

Parkes, Bessie Rayner. Remarks on the education of girls. 1854.

Pennington, Sarah, lady. An unfortunate mother's advice to her absent daughters. 1761 (several editions till 1817).

Pfeiffer, Emily. Women and work ... relation to health and physical development of the higher education. 1888.

Pipe, H. E. Stoddart, Anna M. Life and letters of Hannah E. Pipe (1831-96). 1908.

Remarks on female education adapted particularly to the regulation of schools. 1823.

Sewell, Elizabeth Missing. Principles of education drawn from Nature and Revelation. 2 vols. 1865.

—— Autobiography: edited by Sewell, E. L. 1907.

Shaen, Margaret Josephine. Memoirs of two sisters, Susanna and Catherine Winkworth. 1908.

Shirreff, Emily Anne Eliza. Intellectual education and its influence on ... women. 1858.

—— The Kindergarten. Principles of Froebel's system and their bearing on the education of women. 1876.

(*See, also,* Grey, Mrs W., *ante.*)

Wakefield, Priscilla. Reflections upon the present condition of the female sex, with suggestions. 1798.

Wollstonecraft, Mary. A vindication of the rights of woman. 1792.

—— Thoughts on the education of daughters. 1797.

Zimmern, Alice. Renaissance of Girls' Education in England. 1898.

(e) *Memoirs*

Almond of Loretto (1832-1903). Life and selection from letters of. By Mackenzie, Robt Jas. 1905.

Arnold, Thomas (1795-1842). Life and correspondence. By Stanley, A. P. 1844.

—— Findlay, J. J. Arnold of Rugby: his school life and contributions to education. Cambridge, 1897.

—— Fitch, Sir J. G. Thomas and Matthew Arnold and their influence on education. 1897.

Bain, Alexander (1818-1903). Autobiography. 1904.

Beattie, Jas (1735-1803). Life and writings. By Sir Wm Forbes of Pitsligo. 2 vols. 1806. (Scots education and the 'Bluestockings.')

Bell, Andrew (1753-1832). Life... comprising the history of... the system of mutual tuition. By Robt and C. C. Southey. 3 vols. 1844.

—— An old educational reformer, Andrew Bell. By Meikeljohn, J. M. D. Edinburgh, 1881.

Bernard, Sir Thomas (1750-1818). Life. By Baker, Jas. 1819.

Birkbeck, George (1776-1841). Memoir and review. By Godard, J. G. 1884.

Bowen, Edward Ernest. Memoir, with essays, songs and verses. By Bowen, Wm Edwd. 1902. (King's College, London, 1852-4. Harrow, 1859-1901.)

Brougham, Henry, lord (1778-1868). Life and times written by himself. 3 vols. Edinburgh, 1871.

Butler, Samuel (1774-1839), headmaster of Shrewsbury School. Life and letters. By Butler, Samuel (his grandson). 2 vols. 1896.

Cooper, Thomas (1805-1892) (the 'moral force Chartist'). Life. By himself. 1872.

Copleston, Edward (1776-1849). Memoir with selections from diary and correspondence. By Coplestone, Wm Jas. 1851.

Dawes, Richard (1793-1867), Dean of Hereford. Biographical notice. By Henry, Wm Chas. 1867.

Day, Thomas (1748-1789), author of Sandford and Merton. Life and writings of. By Blackman, John. 1862.

Drane, Augusta Theodosia (1823-1894). A memoir of Mother Francis Raphael (A. T. D.). By Wilberforce, B. A. H. 1895.

Edgeworth, Richard Lovell (1744-1817). Memoirs. 1819.

Edgeworths, The. A study of later eighteenth century education. By Paterson, Alice. 1914.

Ellis, William (1800-1881). Life... with some account of his writings and labours for the improvement of education. By Blyth, E. K. (with a bibliography). 1889.

Fitch, Sir Joshua (1824-1903). An account of the life and work. By Lilley, A. L. 1906.

Fox, Wm Johnson (1786-1864). Life. By Garnett, R. and Garnett, Edwd. 1909.

Gunning, Henry (1780-1854). Reminiscences of... Cambridge from 1780. 2 vols. 1854.

Haig Brown, William (1823-1907) of Charterhouse. Biographical memoir. H. E. Haig Brown (ed.). 1908.

Hill, Frederic (1803-96). An autobiography of fifty years in times of reform. Constance Hill (ed.). 1893.

Hodgson, W. B. (1815-1880). Life and letters. By Meiklejohn, J. M. D. 1883.

Hogg, Quintin (1845–1903). Biography. By Hogg, Ethel M. 1904.

Jones, Sir William (1746–1794). Memoirs of life, writings and correspondence. By Shore, J., lord Teignmouth. 2 vols. 1806. (Harrow, 1753–63, Oxford.)

Lancaster, Joseph (1778–1838). By Salmon, David. 1904.

Lee, Samuel (1783–1852). A scholar of a past generation, a brief memoir of Samuel Lee. By Lee, A. M. 1896.

Lovett, Wm (1800–1877). Life and struggles (by himself). 1876.

Maurice, Frederick Denison (1805–72). Life. Maurice, Sir Frederick. 2 vols. 3rd edn. 1884.

—— Founder of the Working Men's College. By Alford, B. H. 1909.

Owen, Robert (1771–1858). Life ... written by himself, with selections from his writings and correspondence. 1857.

—— Biography. By Podmore, Frank. 2 vols. 1906.

Owen, R. Dale (1801–1877). Threading my way. 1874.

Parr, Samuel (1747–1825). Life, in Works. Ed. Johnstone, John. 8 vols. 1828.

—— Memoirs. By Field, Wm. 2 vols. 1828. (Harrow, 1752–61, 1767–71, Cambridge.)

Pattison, Mark. Memoirs. 1885.

Pestalozzi, J. H. (1746–1827). Memoir. By Mayo, Chas. 2nd edn. 1828. (Lecture delivered in 1826.)

Pitt, Wm (1708–1778), 1st earl of Chatham. Letters to his nephew T. Pitt, then at Cambridge (1751–7). 2nd edn. 1804.

Place, Francis (1771–1854). Life. By Wallas, Graham. 1898.

Priestley, Joseph (1733–1804). Memoirs ... to 1795, written by himself. Continuation by his son J. P. 1805. *See, post,* ii.

Pryme, Geo. (1781–1868). Autobiographical recollections. Ed. Bayne, A. Cambridge, 1870.

Quick, Robert Hebert (1831–1891). Life and remains. By Storr, Francis. 1899.

Sidgwick, Henry. A memoir by A. and E. M. Sidgwick. 1906.

Stow, David (1793–1864), founder of the Training System. Memoir. By Fraser, Wm. 1868.

Stuart, Jas (1843–1913). Reminiscences. 1911.

Temple, Fdk, archbishop (1821–1902). Rugby Memoir, 1857–69: Francis Elliot Kitchener. 1907.

Thring, Edward (1821–1887). Life, Diary and Letters. By Parkin, Sir Geo. R. 1900.

—— A Memory of. By Skrine, Huntley. 1889.

Trimmer, Sarah (1741–1810). Some account of the life and writings, with original letters. 2 vols. 1814.

Wakefield, Gilbert. Memoirs of his life written by himself. 1792.

Watson, Richard (bishop of Llandaff). Anecdotes of the life of Bishop Watson, by himself. 2nd ed. 2 vols. 1818.

(f) Official documents

Shadwell, Lionel Lancelot. Enactments in Parliament specially concerning the Universities of Oxford and Cambridge, the colleges and halls and the colleges of Winchester, Eton and Westminster. 4 vols. Oxf. Hist. Soc. 1912. (Edward III–George V.)

Society for bettering the condition ... of the Poor. Reports, 1802–11, 5 vols.

Reports. Select Committee, to inquire into the education of the lower orders. (Brougham's Committee.) 12 parts. 1816–18.

Reports. Royal Commission to inquire c. charities for education of the Poor. (Lord Brougham's Commission.) 44 vols. 1818–42.
—— Royal Commission into state of universities and colleges of Scotland. 4 vols. 1837.
—— Central Society of Education. 2 vols. 1837–8.
—— Committee on providing useful education for the poorer classes. 1838.
Educational Record, The, of the British and Foreign School Society. 1848, etc.
Report of Royal Commission on the state, discipline, studies and revenues of the university and colleges of Oxford. 2 pts. 1852.
—— on the state etc. of Cambridge. 2 pts. 1853.
Report of Committee on state of education in... Manchester and Salford, etc. 2 pts. 1852–3.
Report of Royal Commission on... popular education in England. (Newcastle Commission.) 6 vols. 1861. (Incl. reports by Fraser, Jas, Arnold and Pattison.)
—— to inquire into revenues and management of certain colleges and schools, and the studies pursued. (Public Schools or Clarendon Commission.) 4 vols. 1864.
—— on the schools in Scotland. (Argyll Commission.) 10 pts. 1865–7.
—— on education given in schools in England. (Schools Inquiry or Taunton Commission.) 21 vols. 1868. (Arnold, M. in Vol. vi.)
—— Schools Inquiry Commission on Technical Education. 1867.
Report of the Lords' Committee on safeguards for the maintenance of religious instruction and worship... in Oxford, Cambridge and Durham. 4 pts. 1870–1.
Report of Royal Commission on the property and income of Oxford and Cambridge. 3 vols. 1873.
—— on technical instruction. Preliminary, 1882. Second report. 5 vols. 1884.
—— on the working of the elementary education acts. (Cross Commission.) 10 vols. 1886–8.
—— on advancement of higher education in London. 1889.
—— Gresham University of London. 3 vols. 1894.
—— on secondary education. (Bryce Commission.) 9 vols. 1895.
Report of a conference on secondary education held in Oxford. Oxford, 1893.
Special Reports on Educational Subjects. 1896 etc.
University of London Act. 1898.
Report of Royal Commission on University Education in London. 1913.

II. Particular Writers

Aikin, John (1747–1822) and Aikin, Anne Letitia (1743–1825), afterwards Barbauld. Evenings at home... for the amusement and instruction of young people. 6 vols. 1792–1796.
Allen, William (1770–1843), editor. The Philanthropist. 1811.
Arnold, Matthew. Reports on elementary schools, 1852–1882. 1889. Popular education of France, with notices of that of Holland and Switzerland. (Report to Newcastle Commission.) 1861. Schools and Universities on the Continent. (Report to Schools Inquiry Commission.) 1868. Friendship's Garland. 1871. A French Eton, or middle class education and the State. 1892. Higher Schools and Universities in Germany. (Report to Schools Inquiry Commission.) 1882. Special Report on... elementary education in Germany, Switzerland and France [Cd–4752]. 1886.
    Huxley, Leonard (ed.). Thoughts on Education chosen from the writings of Matthew Arnold. 1912.
Arnold, Thomas. Miscellaneous Works. 1845. Sermons. 3 vols. 1850–3.

Bain, Alexander (1818–1903). Education as a science. 1879. English composition and rhetoric. 1866. On teaching English. 1887.

Baines, Sir Edward (1800–1890). Letters written to the Rt Hon. Lord John Russell. 1846. An alarm to the Nation on the...measure of State education. 1847. On the progress and efficiency of voluntary education. 1848. Strictures on the new Government measure. 1853. National education. 1856. Our past educational improvement. 1857. Voluntary and religious education. 1857.

Bamford, R. W. Essays on the discipline of children, particularly as regards their education. 1822.

Barnes, Thomas. A brief comparison of...arguments in favour of public and private education. (Memoirs of Lit. and Phil. Soc., Manchester, vol. II. Warrington, 1785.) A plan for the improvement and extension of liberal education in Manchester. (*ibid.*) A discourse delivered at the commencement of the Manchester Academy. Warrington, 1786.

Barrow, William (1754–1836). An essay on education...particularly the merits and defects of the discipline and instruction in our academies. 2 vols. 1802.

Beattie, James (1735—1803). Essays. Edinburgh, 1778. Including Essay on the utility of classical learning (1769).

Beattie, Jas. The Grammarian: or the English writer and speaker's assistant. 1838.

Bell, Andrew. Elements of Tuition. Part III. Ludus Literarius, the classical and grammar school. 1815. The wrongs of children. 1819.

Bentham, Jeremy. Works. Ed. Bowring, J. 11 vols. Edinburgh, 1843. Papers relative to codification and public instruction (in vol. IV). Chrestomathia (in vol. VIII). Memoirs and correspondence (in vols. X, XI).

Bernard, Sir Thomas (1750–1818). Of the education of the Poor. 1809. The new school; an attempt to illustrate its principles, details and advantages. 1809. The Barrington School. 1812.

Blair, Hugh. Lectures on rhetoric and belles lettres. 3 vols. 1817.

Booth, James (1806–1878). Education and educational institutions considered with reference to...the present state of society. 1846. On the influence of examination as an instrument of education. 1854. On the female education of the industrial classes. 1855. Systematic instruction and periodical examination. 1857.

Brougham, Henry Peter, (baron Brougham and Vaux). Letter to Romilly, Sir Samuel. 1818. (The Pamphleteer, vol. XIII.) Speech on the education of the Poor, June, 1820. (The Pamphleteer, vol. XVI; Hansard, vol. II, pp. 49–89.) Inaugural discourse on being installed Lord Rector of Glasgow University. 1825.

 M.A. Queen's College, Oxford. A letter to Henry Brougham... on the best method of restoring decayed grammar schools. 1818. (The Pamphleteer, vol. XIII.)

 Ireland, John. A letter to Henry Brougham. 1819. (The Pamphleteer, vol. XIV.)

Brown, John. An estimate of the manners and principles of the times, 1757–8. An explanatory defence of the estimate etc. 1758. Sermons on various subjects. 1764. (Three on 'the first principles of education.') On the female character and education...with an appendix relative to a proposed code of education. 1765. Thoughts on Civil Liberty, on Licentiousness and Faction. Newcastle, 1765.

Burgh, James (1714–1775). Thoughts on education. 1747.

Burnet, G. Bishop Gilbert Burnet as Educationist, being his Thoughts on Education. Notes and life by John Clarke. Aberdeen, 1900.

A gentleman of Bristol [S. Butler]. An essay upon education intended to show that the common method is defective ... With a plan of a new method. [1753.]

Campbell, Geo. The Philosophy of Rhetoric. 2 vols. 1776.

Central Society of Education: by various authors. Publications. 3 vols. 1837-1839, all published.

Chapman, George (1723-1806). A treatise on education. Edinburgh, 1773.

Chesterfield, Stanhope, Philip Dormer, earl of. Letters of the earl of Chesterfield to his son. 1774-87. *Idem.* Introduction by Strachey, C., notes by Calthrop, A. 1901. Letters to his godson and successor. With appendix, Letters to A. C. Stanhope. Ed. by the earl of Carnarvon. Oxford, 1890.

Colquhoun, John Campbell (1803-1870). On the measures to be now taken ... to secure a good national education. 1853. Memorandum on a bill to make further provision for education ... in Scotland. 1854. Remarks on Pakington's Education Bill. 1855.

Colquhoun, Patrick (1745-1820). A new and appropriate system of education for the labouring people. 1806.

Combe, George (1788-1858). What should secular education embrace? 1847. Remarks on national education. 1847. Lectures on popular education. 1848. Education: its principles and practice as developed by George Combe: collated and edited by Wm Jolly. 1875.

Cornish, Joseph (1750-1823). An attempt to display the importance of classical learning. With some candid remarks on Mr Knox's Liberal Education. 1783.

Creighton, Mandell, bp of London (1843-1901). Thoughts on education. 1902.

Crosby Hall Lectures on Education. 1848.

Dalton, John (1766-1844). Elements of English grammar. 1801.

Dawes, Richard, dean of Hereford. Hints on National Education. 1848. Observations on the working of the government scheme of education. 1849. Suggestive hints towards improved secular instruction, making it bear on practical life. 3rd edn. [1849.] Remarks occasioned by the present crusade against the ... Committee of Council on Education. 1850. Schools and other similar institutions for the industrial classes. 1853. Remarks on the reorganisation of the Civil Service and its bearing on educational progress. 1854. Teaching of common things. 1854. Address to the Huddersfield Mechanics' Institute. [1856.] Mechanics' Institutes and popular education. 1856. Manual of educational requirements for the Civil Service. With a preface on its educational value and importance. 1856. Effective primary instruction the only sure road to success in ... secondary instruction. 1857.

Dunn, Henry (Secretary, Br. and For. School Soc.). Popular education. 1837. National education, the question of questions. 1838. Calm Thoughts on the recent Minutes of the Committee of Council. 1847.

Edgeworth, Maria, and Richard L. Practical Education. 2 vols. 1798.

Edgeworth, Richard Lovell. Essays on professional education. 1809. Poetry explained for young people. 1802. Early Lessons. New ed. 1815.

Edgeworth, Maria. The Parent's Assistant or Stories for Children. Pt I. 2nd edn. 1796. 3rd edn. 6 vols. 1800. 1897 edn (selections) in 1 vol.; introduction by Ritchie, Anne Thackeray.

Edinburgh Review, The. The English universities and public schools: Nos. xxii (1808): xxviii, xxix (1809): xxxi, xxxii (1810). Elementary education: Nos. i (1802): xvii (1806); xxi (1807); xxxiii, xxxvii (1811). General: Nos. ix (1804); xiii (1805); xvii, xxx, xl.

Ensor, George (1769-1843). On rational education. 1811.

Enfield, William (1741–1797). The Speaker. 1774. An essay on the cultivation of taste as a proper object...in education. 1818.

Farrar, Fdk Wm (editor). Essays on a liberal education. 1867. (C. S. Parker, H. Sidgwick, J. Seeley, E. E. Bowen, F. W. Farrar, J. M. Wilson, J. W. Hales, W. Johnson, Lord Houghton.)

Fawcett, Henry and Millicent Garrett. Essays and lectures on social and political subjects. Cambridge, 1872. Contains 3 essays on educational subjects, all by M. G. F.

Fitch, Sir Joshua Girling (1824–1903). Public education. Why is a new code wanted? 1861. Charity Schools and the Endowed Schools Commission. 1873. Lectures on Teaching. 1881. Notes on American schools and training colleges. 1890. Educational aims and methods. 1900.

Fox, Joseph. A comparative view of the plans of... Dr Bell and Mr Lancaster. 1808. Scriptural education the glory of England, a defence of the Lancastrian plan. 1810.

Fraser, Jas (Bishop of Manchester, 1818–1885). The Revised Code. 1861.

Genlis, Stéphanie Félicité de. Adèle et Théodore. 3 vols. Maestricht, 1782.

Gilkes, Arthur H. A day at Dulwich. 1905.

Gill, John (1818–1910). Systems of Education: a history and criticism. 1876.

Godwin, William. Enquiry concerning political justice. 2 vols. 1793. See Bk VI, esp. chap. VIII. The Enquirer; reflections on education, manners and literature. 1797. *See* Pt I, Essay IX.

Grey, Mrs Wm (Maria Georgina Shirreff). The education of women. 1871. The study of education as a science. Paper read at the British Association, Belfast. 1874.

  See, ante, I (*d*) *and also, post,* Shirreff, Emily A. E.

Hamilton, Richard Winter (1794–1848). Institutions of popular education. Leeds. 1846.

Harrison, George. Some remarks relative to the present state of education among...the Quakers. 1802.

Hill, Arthur, Hill, Frederic, Hill, Matthew Davenport (1792–1872). Hill, Sir Rowland (1795–1879). Public education: plans for the government of boys as practised at Hazelwood School. 1822. New ed. 1894. The Laws of Hazelwood School. 1827. Sketch of the system of education at the schools of Bruce Castle, Tottenham, and Hazelwood, near Birmingham. 1833. *See, also,* Geo. Birkbeck Hill. Life of Sir Rowland Hill. 2 vols. 1880.

Hodgson, Wm Ballantyne (1815–1880). On the report of the [Public Schools] Commissioners. 1864. On the education of girls considered in connexion with the university local examinations. 1864. Exaggerated estimates of reading and writing as means of education. 1868. Education of girls and employment of women of the upper classes. 2nd. 1869. The importance of the study of economic science. 1870.

Home, Henry, Lord Kames. Loose Hints upon Education, chiefly concerning the culture of the heart. Edinburgh, 1781. Elements of rhetoric. 1762.

Hume, David. Essays and treatises on several subjects. New edn. 1758. *See* essays XVI Of eloquence, and XXVI Of the standard of taste (both published in 1742).

Huxley, Thos. Henry (1825–1895). Science and Education: vol. III of Collected Essays. 1893–1894.

Ingram, Robert Acklom (1763–1809). A sermon preached in Colchester for the benefit of the Charity School. Colchester. 1788. Parochial benefi-

cence inculcated: the school of industry, Boxted. Colchester. [1800.]
An essay on...schools of industry and religious instruction. London,
[1808].

Johnson, Samuel. Plan of a dictionary of the English language. 1747.

Kay, Joseph (1821–1878). Education of the poor in England and Europe.
1846. Social conditions and education of the people in England and
Europe. 2 vols. 1850. The condition and education of poor children
in English and German towns. 1853.

Kay-Shuttleworth, Sir James Phillips. The school in its relation to the
State, the Church and the congregation. 1847. Public education from
1846–52. 1853. Letter to Earl Granville on the Revised Code. 1861.
Four Periods of Public Education, 1832–1839–1846–1862. 1862. Memorandum on the present state of the question of popular education.
[1868.]

Kingsley, Charles (1819–1875). Health and Education. 1874.

Knox, Vicesimus (1752–1821). Works: with biographical preface. 7 vols.
1824. Essays, moral and literary. Vol. I, 1778; vol. II, 1779. Frequently
reprinted: new ed. 3 vols. 1823. Liberal education: or, a practical
treatise on...acquiring useful and polite learning. 1781. Letter to...
Lord North, Chancellor of the University of Oxford. 1789. (In 10th ed.
of Liberal Education.) Personal nobility or letters to a young nobleman
on the conduct of his studies. 1793. Remarks on the tendency of...a
bill now pending...to degrade grammar schools. 2nd edn. 1821. (The
Pamphleteer, vol. XIX.)

Lancaster, Henry Hill (1829–1875). Essays and Reviews: prefatory notice
by Benj. Jowett. Edinburgh, 1876.

Lancaster, Joseph. Improvements in education as it respects the industrious
classes. 1803.

    See, also, ante, I (*a*) and (*e*).

Latham, Henry. On examinations as a means of selection. Cambridge,
1877.

Laurie, Simon Somerville (1829–1909). John Amos Comenius: life and
educational works. 3rd edn. 1887. Lectures on the rise...of universities, with a survey of mediaeval education. 1886. Occasional
addresses on educational subjects. 1888. Institutes of Education. 1892.
Historical survey of pre-Christian education. 1895. Studies in the
history of educational opinion. 1903.

[Louth, Robert.] A short introduction to English grammar. 1762.

Lowe, Robert, viscount Sherbrooke (1811–1892). Primary and classical education. Edinburgh, 1867. Middle class education: endowment or
free-trade? 1868.

Macnab, Henry Grey (1761–1823). A plan of reform in the mode of instruction. Glasgow, 1786. Analysis and analogy recommended...in education.
Paris, 1818.

    See, also, post, Owen, Robert.

Mann, Horace. Report of an educational tour in Germany and parts of
Great Britain and Ireland. Preface by Hodgson, W. B. 1846.

Martineau, James (1805–1900). Essays and Addresses.

Martineau, Harriet (1802–76). How to observe. 1838. Household Education. 1849. Autobiography. 1877.

Maurice, John Frederick Denison. Has the Church or State power to
educate the Nation? 1839. National education. A sermon. 1853.
The workman and the franchise; chapters from English history on the
representation and education of the people. 1866.

    See, also, ante, I (*a*), (*b*) Oxford, and (*e*).

Maxse, Fdk Augustus (1833–1900). The education of the agricultural poor. 1868. National education and its opponents. 1877.

Mayo, Charles (1792–1846). Observations on the establishment and direction of infant schools. 1826.

Mill, James (1773–1836). Education *in* Encycl. Brit. Supplement. 1824.
—— State of the Nation. Westminster Review, October. 1826.

Mill, John Stuart. Inaugural Address, St Andrews University. 1867.

More, Hannah. Thoughts on the importance of the manners of the great to general society. 1788. Remarks on the speech of M. Dupont...on religion and public education. 1793.
   See, also, ante, I (*d*).

Murray, Lindley. English grammar adapted to different classes of learners. York, 1795.

Museum and English Journal of Education, The. 5 vols. 1864–9.

Nelson, James (1710–94). An essay on the government of children. 1753.

One of practical experience. Remarks on popular education in reference to the New Code. Bradford, 1861.

Owen, Robert. A new view of Society, or essays on...the formation of human character. 1813.
   Macnab, Henry Grey. The new views of Mr Owen...impartially examined. 1819.

Owen, Robert Dale. Outlines of the new system of education at New Lanark. 1824.

Paine, Thomas. The Rights of Man. 1st part, 1791, 2nd part, 1792.

Payne, Joseph (1808–1876). The true foundation of science teaching. 1873. The science and art of education. 1874. Pestalozzi: influence on elementary education. 1875. Fröbel and the Kindergarten. 1876. A visit to German schools. 1876. Lectures on the science and art of education. 1883.

Pillans, James. Principles of elementary teaching, chiefly in reference to the parochial schools of Scotland. Edinburgh, 1828. Three lectures. 1836. A word for the universities of Scotland. Edinburgh, 1848. The rationale of discipline as exemplified in the High School. Edinburgh, 1852. Contributions to the cause of education. 1856. Educational papers read before the Education Department of the Social Science Assoc. Edinburgh, 1862.

Place, Francis (1771–1854). Improvement of the Working People. 1834.

Price, Richard (1723–1791). The evidence for a future improvement in... mankind. 1787.

Priestley, Joseph. An essay on the first principles of government. 1768 (esp. Pt II, Section II). An essay on a course of liberal education for civil and active life (1764), *in* Miscellaneous observations relating to education. Bath, 1778. The proper objects of education. 1791. The rudiments of English grammar: a course of lectures on the theory of language and universal grammar,...; and lectures on oratory and criticism. Notes and appendix by J. T. Rutt. 1826. (Three separate works written between 1761 and 1768.)

Quarterly Review, The. Vols. V, VI, VIII, XIV, XV, XVI, XXXII, XXXVII, XXXIX— chiefly on elementary education.

Quick, Robert Hebert (1831–1891). Essays on educational reformers. 1868.
   Positions, by Richard Mulcaster, with an...account of his life and writings. 1888.

Robertson, Chas. Objections to a system of free education for the people. n.d.

Roby, Henry John (1830-1915). Remarks on College reform. 1858. The present state of the schools: the law of charities as affecting endowed schools: chps II, IV of the Endowed Schools Report. 1867.

> *See, also,* Memoirs of Archbishop Temple, by seven Friends. 1906.

Rogers, Wm (1819-1896). Reminiscences: compiled by R. H. Hadden. 1888.

Rooper, Thos. Godolphin (1847-1903). A pot of green feathers. School and home life. 1896. Selected writings: ed. with a memoir by R. G. Tatton. 1907.

Ruskin, John. *See* Camb. Hist. Eng. Lit., vol. XIV, bibliography to chap. III.

> Jolly, Wm. Ruskin on Education, some needed but neglected elements. 1894.

Seeley, Sir John. English in Schools *in* Lectures and Essays. 1895.

Sewell, Wm (1804-1874). An essay on the cultivation of the intellect by the study of the dead languages. 1830. A speech...at the meeting of friends of national education at Willis's Rooms, Feb. 7th. 1850.

Shaw, William (Rector of Chelvey, Somerset). Suggestions respecting national education. Bath, 1801.

Sheppard, J. G. Remarks on the Rev. F. Temple's scheme for the extension of middle-class education. 1857.

Sheridan, Thomas. British Education. In three parts. 1756. A general view of the scheme for the improvement of education. [Dublin, 1758.] A dissertation on the causes of the difficulties...in learning the English tongue. 1762. A course of lectures on elocution. 1762. A plan of education for the young nobility and gentry. 1769. Lectures on the art of reading. 2 vols. 1775. A general dictionary of the English language...to establish a plain and permanent standard of pronunciation. To which is prefixed a rhetorical grammar. 2 vols. 1780. A short address to the Public. 1783.

> Proceedings of the Hibernian Society. Dublin, 1758.
>
> A letter to a schoolmaster...relative to Mr Sheridan's scheme of education. Dublin, 1758.
>
> An enquiry into the plan and pretensions of Mr Sheridan. Dublin 1758.
>
> A true history of the scheme for erecting a new seminary. Dublin, 1769.
>
> An examen of Mr Sheridan's plan. 1784.

Shirreff, Emily Anne Eliza (1814-1897). Thoughts on self-culture (with her sister, Maria Georgina). 2 vols. 1850. Intellectual education and its influence on...women. 1858. The Kindergarten: also, remarks on the higher education of women. 1876.

Smith, Adam. An enquiry into the nature and causes of the wealth of nations. 1776. Bk V, chp. I, articles II, III.

Smith, Sydney. Works. 2 vols. 1859.

> *See* contributions to the Edinburgh Review.

Spencer, Herbert. Education, intellectual, moral and physical. 1861. Very frequently rptd.

> Compayré, Gabriel. H. Spencer et l'éducation scientifique. Paris, [1901.]

Stockdale, Percival (1736-1811). An examination...whether education at a great school or by private tuition is preferable. With remarks on Mr Knox's Liberal Education. 1782.

[Taylor, Isaac, 1787-1865.] Home education. 2nd edn. 1838.

Teacher, An experienced. The complete governess; a course of mental instruction for ladies. 1826.

Temple, Frederick, archbishop of Canterbury. On apprenticeship and school. 1858. Sermons preached in Rugby School Chapel in 1858, 1859, 1860. Series 1–3, 1861–71. National schools. 1870. The true ideal of the educator. 1898.

Thelwall, John. Selections for the illustration of a course of instructions on the rhythmus and utterance of the English language. 1812.

Thompson, D'Arcy Wentworth. Day dreams of a schoolmaster. Edinburgh, 1864. Wayside Thoughts: desultory essays on education. 1868.

Thring, Edward. Education and School. 1864. Theory and practice of teaching. 1883. Sermons preached at Uppingham School. 2 vols. 1886. Addresses. 1887. Poems and translations. 1887.

Todhunter, Isaac (1820–84). The conflict of studies and other essays connected with education. 1873.

Trimmer, Sarah. The Oeconomy of charity. 1786. Reflections upon the education of children in charity schools. 1792. A comparative view of the new plan of education promulgated by Mr Joseph Lancaster. 1805. The Guardian of Education, a periodical work. 5 vols. 1802–1806. An essay on Christian education. 1812.

Tuer, Andrew White (1838–1900). History of the Hornbook. 2 vols. 1896. Pages and Pictures from Forgotten Children's Books. 1898.

Watts, John, Ph.D. (1818–1887). On national education considered as a question of political and financial economy. 1850.

Whately, Richard, archbishop of Dublin (1787–1863). Rhetoric: rptd from the ...Encyclop. Metrop. 1828.

Whitchurch, Jas Wadham. An essay upon education. 1772.

Wilderspin, Samuel. On the importance of educating the infant poor. 1824. Early discipline. 1840. System for the education of the young.

Williams, A. M. The Scottish School of Rhetoric. 1897.

Williams, David (1738–1816), founder of the R. Literary Fund. A treatise upon education. 1774.

Wordsworth, Wm. The Prelude (1799–1805). 1850. The Excursion: Bks 8 and 9: with Wordsworth's note in the 1843 edition.
　　Jas Fotheringham. Wordsworth's 'Prelude' as a study in education. 1899.

Wyse, Sir Thos (1791–1862). Education reform, or the necessity of a national system. 1836.

Wyse, W. M. Notes on education reform in Ireland from ... the unpublished memoirs of ... Sir Thomas Wyse. Waterford, 1901.

Yates, Jas (1789–1871). Thoughts on the advancement of academical education in England. 1826. Outlines of a constitution for the university of London. 1832.

43/100

III. Unpublished Material

Place MSS.: Br. Mus. Additional MSS. 27823, 27824 contain papers, printed and manuscript, and letters relating to Joseph Lancaster, Lancasterian and "Chrestomathic" schools, mechanics' institutes and the foundation of London university.

PRINTED IN GREAT BRITAIN
BY W. LEWIS
AT THE CAMBRIDGE UNIVERSITY PRESS